"*Bounce Back! is not only an easy, enjoyable read—it's useful too!*"
Dave Broadfoot, Comedian

"*There's a lot of pain in selling. This book will help you bounce back from the inevitable disappointments all salespeople experience and reach higher levels of success.*"
Mike Stewart, CSP
International Sales Trainer

"*A practical and inspirational book of real people with much to teach us all. I will keep this book close at hand for those times when I need to get myself back on track.*"
Judith Tobin, Partner
Beleto International Inc.

"*Bounce Back! is a very uplifting book with great stories to remind us that life is worth living.*"
Ann Clancy, Marketing Manager,
Wilson Smith Learning Resources

"*This book touched my soul; it's a gift I'll be sharing with friends and colleagues.*"
Lori Dalton, Relationship Manager,
IBM Canada

"*If you want to discover the essential secrets for experiencing a richer life and heightened joy you must immediately settle into your favourite chair and devour Bounce Back! Your future will become instantly brighter!*"

Glenna Salsbury CSP, CPAE*, Speaker and
Author, *The Art of the Fresh Start*

"*Here's a book for those who want to develop the resilience to go beyond surviving to thriving in a world of constant change.*"

Terry Paulson, PhD, CSP, CPAE
Vice-President, NSA, Speaker and Author

"*Bounce Back!, with humour and sensitivity, takes us on an intimate journey toward hope.*"

Jim Harris, Speaker and Author

"*It's a great book. I think you should buy it.*"

Jonathan Nelson, Kid

*(CSP-Certified Speaking Professional; CPAE-Council of Peers Award for Excellence as recognized by the National Speakers' Association)

# BOUNCE Back!

## Creating resilience from adversity

**Reva Nelson**

Author of *Risk It!*

Nelson, Reva, *Bounce Back! Creating Resilience from Adversity*, Words•Worth Professional Communications, Toronto, 1997.

**Canadian Cataloguing in Publication Data**
Nelson, Reva, 1948—
    Bounce Back

Includes bibliographical references.
ISBN: 0-9695410-1-5

1.    Life change events - Psychological aspects.
2.    Adjustment (Psychology). I. Title.

BF637.L53N44 1997  158.1  C97-930773-2

**Production**
*Editor:*    June Rogers
*Cover:*    Mahmoud Ramezani
*Design:*    BG Communications
*Printer:*    Webcom
*Photo:*    Gordon Theo

# Author's note

I love a good story. I'm fascinated by people's histories; I learn from them. The questions always lurking on my mind are "How did you ever get through it? What did you do when that crisis hit? How did you handle that?" What happened with this work on resilience is that I became engrossed with the people who talked with me about some of their most painful times because they were so open. Even though I've researched this topic of resilience since 1989, and the statistics, facts, understanding and knowledge are incorporated into my seminars, that's not how this book evolved into being. It seemed to take on a life of its own, which is in the lives of all of us who have had to become resilient in one way or another.

Life can be wonderful, or not; there are times when it's just plain difficult and precarious. The people I spoke with touched me. I hope to touch you, and help you. It's their book as much as mine, and I thank them for their honesty and candor.

PER ARDUA AD ASTRA
(Through adversity to the stars)

## Dedication

For my mother and in loving memory of my father.

To single parents, and to those unfortunate enough to have to deal with chronic diseases or pain who still manage to smile and ask "How's your day going?"

## Special thanks to

The friends who encouraged me to keep writing, especially Riça Night, Colin Watson, Angela Jackson and Tom Doris.

People who read the rough drafts and offered valuable feedback, especially Lynn Marshall and Terry Paulson.

Fellow NSA & CAPS members, my family and friends and always,

My kid, Jonathan, for reminding me about what's important and for keeping me laughing.

## In appreciation of the interviewees

Franka Baptiste, Eli Bay, Les Beach, Kay Brett, Terry Crowe, Charlene Day, Steve Donahue, John Easton, Deb Filler, Angela Jackson, Dawn Laverdure, Steve Levine, Sheila Levy, Stuart Macdonald, Edna Manitouwabi, Jean Marmoreo, Charlene Marshall, Caroline Middleton, Catherine Mossop, Neil Muscott, Don Myles, Martin Rutte, Hubert St. Onge, John Woods, Beverly Zucker

# Table of Contents

# Introduction

We all need to be more like Silly Putty. Do you remember that toy? Since I was a kid, I've loved Silly Putty. It's stretchy, bouncy, stringy and smooth. You can put it on the comics, transfer the image of a cartoon face, and stretch it around to make a new funny face. It sits in a plastic egg case just waiting to come out and play. When you roll it into a ball and bounce it, it bounces back. It's resilient. Personally and professionally, we can learn a lot from this magical toy.

There are so many difficult changes to face, such as a failed marriage, a death in the family, kids in trouble, an injury or a serious illness. Workplace problems include a job loss (your own or your colleague's), low morale, bad press, product line changes, lack of trust, uncertainty, internal communication problems, fewer resources, role confusion, no fun, lack of vision and direction, no leadership and an unreasonable workload! So, the ability to bounce back, to be resilient, like silly putty, is necessary.

In my work, leading workshops and speaking at conferences, I deal with the inner self and the organizational self. A colleague asked, regarding this book on resilience, "Is this a business book or a self-help book?" I don't see the two as separate from each other. I've often been intrigued with what happens to people at work. To me, if you are miserable at home, you can't be happy at work, and vice versa. One may be an escape from the other, but the ideal—I do always look for the ideal—is an integrated self. You are able to express yourself and your creativity at work, and you are stronger and happier at home, because of your work.

My background is in education, theatre and business. In 1980, I left teaching and the theatre to lead workshops for parents, people in transition and the career centre of a university, respectively. I didn't really know much about corporations or life inside the organization, but I learned quickly as the size and nature of my client list grew. I met some vibrant, enthusiastic people who loved life and their work. Most were not like that, however. Most people seemed frustrated by the lack of input and involvement they could have in their work.

While I was leading several government workshops, I was offered a position with one Ministry. The first thing that popped out of my mouth was, "What? Sell my soul?" (Perhaps a slight exaggeration.) My perception was that most people in organizations were terribly unhappy, except for their paycheques. They seemed stuck, bought by the pension plan. This was in 1983, and not many were considering leaving. They didn't know that 10 years later, several would be pretty much forced to leave, to "retire early." I saw a great deal of pain, and began to reflect on "corporate hurt." I thought then I'd write a book about "corporate healing," but instead went on to write the *Risk It!*

book, which is, in a sense, still about healing, about taking action to make a vision come true. It's about involvement, by choice, with your life and work.

However, the notion of Resilience was born for me, at that time. As with most notions or intuitive insights that I have, it grabbed onto my pant leg like a puppy and wouldn't let go. I had the idea that we couldn't have corporate health without having inner health. I wondered how an organization gets stronger. Some people think it's by changing the structure. I agree that works in some situations. But just changing the structure without changing the mindsets of the people will not lead to an effective outcome.

> For outer strength, for strong companies that can compete globally, we need inner strength.

We need people who have the ability to stretch beyond usual boundaries and convictions about their work and what they can offer. We need people who can continue to believe in their value and worth, no matter what happens externally to them or their company. One of the problems is that more and more people are feeling the stress of the change, not realizing that bouncing back is expected, required and a healthy response to the stress.

Twelve years ago, my marriage ended. It wasn't my choice at that time. My relationship to my ex-husband deteriorated to the point of no contact at all. I moved to Toronto with my son who was not quite two. I had two business contracts, and one fell through. My ex-husband was an artist; I was an independent consultant. Even though I had very little money, I spent it all to buy a small house. It was a third of the size we'd had and cost twice the money.

One weekend I had only six dollars to buy the groceries with. I took my toddler shopping, gave him dinner, played with him, put him to bed, and cried the rest of the weekend. A neighbour, knowing I was self-employed and new to the city, asked, sort of jokingly, how I was doing and whether or not I needed a food basket. My embarrassment and pride wouldn't allow me to say yes. I was educated, I came from a decent home, this was not supposed to be my life.

My house had surprises. The roof leaked so badly in the first rain storm that I had buckets in the bedrooms until I could borrow the money for repairs. Then I discovered the house had tenants—non-paying mice and cockroaches. I moved them out, cleaned up, moved a paying tenant in, and we struggled as I tried to rebuild my business and my life. A friend encouraged me by saying, "You'll get through this, Reva. You're one of the most resilient people I know." His image of me was that of a ship that had been smashed about through the waves, but would not sink. I would emerge as a sleeker, stronger, more resilient vessel than ever. I drew a picture of his image and it stays on my bulletin board still.

There were many days I felt like flotsam on the seas. Forget the emerging sleeker scenario. I ate President's Choice decadent chocolate chip cookies by the bag. This was my idea of soul food. One friend said, "Put them in the freezer, you won't be so tempted." That worked until another friend asked if I'd ever tried them right out of the freezer. Truly delicious, what a great discovery.

The next few years were very difficult. What got me through was the need to be a responsible parent, to put food on the table and to make a joyful home for my child. I had to learn to allow the support of my neighbours, family, friends and colleagues, who came through in so many ways. I couldn't have survived without their humour and help. I also found that I was tremendously inspired by the books of others who'd been through tough times, and the stories I often read in the paper of individual struggles. There were so many amazing people who had tremendous adversity to overcome. Their wisdom and truth were so inspirational to me.

I began to reflect on resilience more and more. Why is it that some people lose it over the smallest thing? This woman breaks a nail and her day is ruined. That man is kept waiting for a table at a restaurant and practically goes up in a smoke of rage. Why does one company suffer from such low morale, whereas another, with an even worse bottom line, manages to rebuild its teams and starts a full recovery?

The resilience of one friend of mine really stands out. In one year, her father became ill and died, her husband's father became ill and died, her husband lost his job and *she* developed cancer. In the midst of all this, including her three kids and her own business, she called me to ask how *I* was. And I, like a normal person, unthinkingly started to moan about something, and then stopped cold. "What am I doing, complaining to you? Look at all you have to deal with right now." She replied, "That's OK. It helps me to hear about someone else's problems for a change." I was amazed. In the midst of her own private hell, where there was very little she could control, she still was reaching out to others to show concern. Fortunately, she and her family recovered.

I believe the ability to be resilient can be learned. There

are a set of skills that we can practise, plus some stories we can be inspired by. I began to offer a course on resilience along with my other programs. Then I shaped the material into a keynote speech. It's working. What I've been told most often about my resilience programs over the last five years is, "We really needed to hear this." "This information was so timely." "We've been suffering; you've helped ease that and made us believe we can continue." "I needed to hear you for my work life, but most of all, for myself." Many people are really suffering in the depths of uncertainty right now at home and at work.

All of us face tough times, some of us more than others. There are times in our lives when we have recognizable stressors, times of natural change: toddlerhood, teenage years, dating, first (or any) marriage, mid-life changes and the elder years. These are times of normal disruption and re-integration, times of extreme stress, called bifurcation points. They cause a disruption in our usual homeostatic state and can increase our feelings of chaos. If we learn to regroup and reintegrate, we emerge healthy, with new structures. If we don't, we may be attracted to "distractors" such as alcohol or drugs. This is a dysfunctional response. People, and organizations, may have dysfunctional responses. In an organization, there may be a "hunkering down" response, more orders, more rigidity, less room for trial and error, creativity and innovation. For individuals, we too may become more defensive and less able to cope.

With both organizations and individuals, we need to learn responses that will lead away from anger and confusion, toward creativity and strength.

The following pages contain the information I've gleaned from my research, my interviews with other courageous and resilient people, and my own insights. I hope you take it to heart and it helps, whether you're the company president, a manager, a mom or dad, a teenager, or a person with a friend who's in pain right now. If I can help you, my pain has been worth it. If you can help someone else, your pain has been worth it too.

I believe it's a mistake to think of living life only halfway, protecting, safeguarding, not risking. If we can all be more resilient, pliable, stretchable, like silly putty, we can continue to embrace all that life offers. We can learn to bounce back with greater resilience and new found strength.

Life is a dance-partner
Waiting for us to take the first step
And lead with passion and joy.

I encourage you to take the first step.

Reva Nelson
Toronto, Canada

# Ten skills for greater resilience

There are many different ways to look at developing resilience. I have chosen 10 skill areas that, when worked on, lead to a greater ability to be resilient, like silly putty.

The areas are not exclusive of each other at all; in fact they are closely linked. For example, being able to laugh helps our stress level. Visualization requires some creativity too, which also needs some risk-taking ability. However, all of the skills can be developed and worked on in order to lead to a more resilient personality and organization.

1. Keep a sense of humour and perspective.
2. Learn to handle the stress of change.
3. Allow yourself to "deaden," withdraw, feel pain, heal and return again.
4. Deal with the anger.
5. Maintain a positive self-esteem.
6. Visualize a better future.
7. Be creative.
8. Become a resourceful survivor.
9. Take some risks.
10. Keep faith.

"Even though conditions such as lack of sleep, insufficient food and various mental stresses may suggest that the inmates were bound to react in certain ways, in the final analysis it becomes clear that the sort of person the prisoner became was the result of an inner decision, and not the result of camp influences alone. Fundamentally, therefore, any man can, even under such circumstances, decide what shall become of him—mentally and spiritually....Suffering is an ineradicable part of life, even as fate and death. Without suffering and death, human life cannot be complete."

Viktor Frankl, *Man's Search for Meaning*
(regarding Auschwitz concentration camp)

> *"Joking is undignified; that is why it is so good for one's soul."*
>
> G.K. Chesterton

# Skill 1

# Keep a sense of humour and perspective

Gary is a friend of mine who worked for the provincial government, in race relations. It was a very stressful, demanding job. Gary had a loud, hearty laugh that people could hear down the hall and around the corner. He said he knew it was time to leave his job when three different colleagues said, "I never hear you laugh anymore." He was completely stressed and burned out, and laughter wasn't bubbling anywhere near the surface.

Psychiatrists state that one of the first things that changes when we become depressed is our ability to laugh. It's a sign of trouble with the psyche when we can't see the light side at all. We are wallowing in the dark. The ability to laugh, *especially* when we are in pain, eases the pain. Sharing a troublesome time with a friend, and looking at the ridiculous aspects of the situation helps us heal.

When my friend Cheryl's husband left her and their two young children to be with his new girlfriend, she was, of course, devastated. When he didn't pay support, and she worried about feeding the kids, she was even more angry and hurt. At one point, standing at my kitchen counter drinking tea, she said, "He can't pay support—he just bought a new car." Well, that was all it took to get us going. We delved into the absurd immediately, took the ball and ran with it, and made up statements for her ex-husband, such as, "I'm sorry dear, I have to make these Porsche payments." Laughter was the only thing that got us though those times of no child support. (I'm aware that there are ex-husbands who were not treated fairly and also must deal with the rough results from shattered dreams.)

When my aunt Lilly, whom we all loved dearly, was dying of cancer, she stayed in her own home, with nursing care. One time I visited and knocked at her door. Since her hair had fallen out, she answered the door wearing a scarf on her head, looking smaller and more frail than ever. She said "I bet you weren't expecting Mother Teresa." We laughed together and a very awkward moment was passed.

During another visit, when she was even more sick, and lying in the makeshift bedroom off the kitchen, my cousins and I sat around the table and recalled all the silly things we did as kids. We cracked jokes and laughed and laughed. One of the nurses could handle this; the other thought we were quite disrespectful. It's odd to say we had some of our best times laughing around that table, but we did, and I'm sure our laughter was an enjoyable sound to my aunt. It helped ease our pain about losing someone we loved so much.

Humour has found its way into even the most bleak places. Viktor Frankl, psychiatrist and author of *Man's Search for Meaning*, said that even in the Auschwitz concentration camp, humour helped. Fellow inmates joked about their getting so used to hoping for a ladle of the watery soup from the bottom of the pot, where there might be a piece of carrot or potato, that they feared on their release, if they ever got to a fancy dinner party again, they would blurt out to the hostess. "Please, could you ladle the soup from the bottom?" Frankl stated:

"An outsider may be astonished to hear that one could find a sense of humour in a concentration camp... Humour was another of the soul's weapons in the fight for self-preservation... it can afford an aloofness and an ability to rise above any situation, even if only for a few seconds."

Humour enables us to keep a positive perspective on life. It's a release for pain. If we can "look on the bright side," we're getting out of the depths of the dark side, if even for a moment. Many comedians had an unhappy childhood. It's not a prerequisite for successful material, but it helps. They saw they were different, and needed a way to make it all right to not fit in. It's precisely because of the "not fitting in" that they can look at the absurdities of life and comment. Humorists are observers and commentators from the sidelines. If they "fit in," they wouldn't notice what "out" was.

In times of extreme stress and pain, none of us, in fact, fit in. I remember when my father was dying, I'd leave the hospital and walk around downtown in a daze. I felt so distanced from everyone else, and surprised that someone couldn't tell just from looking at me that I'd just come from a near-death at a hospital. I felt totally disconnected from everyone and everything. An old childhood friend called and invited me to a funny movie. We went and laughed, and it helped a tremendous amount. Humour helps bridge the gap; it enables us to re-enter the day-to-day world. Steve Allen states:

"Tragedy + Time = Comedy"

What is humour? Many people think humour means the ability to tell a joke, but that's only one small piece of the humour pie. It's scratching an itch; real humour is a long soak in the tub. Many funny people do not tell jokes well, or may never tell a joke at all, but they sure are funny. They come out with the one-liners, or a look or a comment that can crack you up, but was unplanned.

Other people have a great sense of humour, but they are not that funny themselves. My colleague, Wilson, is pretty deadpan, à la Bob Newhart. But he laughs readily and easily, a very valuable commodity. He appreciates humour more than he generates it, but occasionally he hits home with a one-liner that is hilarious. I love calling him because he laughs at all my jokes.

We all need an audience. My friend Charlene has a laugh that can rattle the windows. One day I'm going to hire her to do nothing more than sit at the back of my seminars and laugh.

I believe everyone has a sense of humour. We like to laugh. Look at babies. It's so easy to get them giggling. Did you ever see a baby when it first discovers its toes? It laughs and laughs and thinks these weird things at the end of its legs are hysterical objects put there for personal amusement. It's also great for the parents, because it's one of the first times the baby can amuse itself long enough for them to make a cup of coffee. Parents and friends will usually be as silly as possible to get the baby to laugh. We can allow ourselves silliness when we feel safe.

Humour researchers don't agree on what humour is, and

whether we're born with it or not, but everyone knows it can be nourished and developed. Basically, it's a willingness to laugh, to look at events sideways and upside down, and to notice why you and others laugh. I never thought of myself as a humourist until a colleague called to say she put my name forward to a client for a keynote speech on humour. I gulped and asked, "Why d'ja do that?" She said, "You're one of the funniest people I know. Surely you could deliver a dynamite speech on humour." (Those who know one of my key workshop topics is Risk-Taking love to hand me a risk on a platter.) Well, I walk every day, but I don't claim to be a physiotherapist. I had, however, already been researching the topic of humour for myself, to bring more humour into my established keynote speeches. I spoke to the potential client, told her where I was in my development of the topic, and together we worked on the results she wanted from the speech. I developed *When Laugh Lines Meet Life Lines: How to laugh at your life and your work when you feel like you can't.* It's been a terrific topic; I've had great fun with it, and it brings into play the same key points with all my topics: Skill, Attitude and Perspective.

However, just learning the skills, without a change of heart, doesn't allow change to happen. People revolt, sabotage, or just plain don't "come on board," whether it's a change in the rules at home, or at work. So shifting their attitude, and helping them learn to look on the funny side of change, is valuable to them and to their organization.

I will caution, though, that sometimes humour can be a dangerous weapon. Even the words of humour imply hurt: I slayed them, I killed them, he stabbed me with his wit. Humour can be a defense mechanism.

There are nine years between myself and my oldest brother, and I was stabbed many times by his sarcasm. I learned to stab back, and could be quite deadly in my comments. I'd try to get him first before he could get me. It wasn't until I started to date that one brave young man told me, "I find your sarcasm really unpleasant and hurtful." This was news to me, but I paid attention and stopped doing it, unless I was with very close friends where the love between us could carry it.

I chose to be careful, because stabbing humour can hurt. Inappropriate humour has no place in meetings or the board room either. How do you know? If you think it could hurt, it's not appropriate. A shared joke is the shortest distance between two people, but a racist, sexist, religious joke can cause real damage. What's allowable between two close friends is different. The old saying about "When in doubt, leave it out" applies to tasteless jokes.

What's left? Anything that makes fun of the basic human condition we all share is safe: early mornings, crying babies, taxes, death, responsibilities, pets, lack of sleep, bills, jobs, teens and car repairs. Not fun stuff, until you can laugh about it.

Mistakes always get a laugh. Recently I did a session on Presentation Skills and Risk-Taking (quite the combination) for the March of Dimes. I related this true story to them:

In 1956, I was eight years old. A lady came to our door to collect for the March of Dimes. My mom was busy upstairs, so I asked her "How much?" She said two, and I thought she meant two dimes, so that's what I gave the lady. Later, I found out she meant two dollars (worth about $20 back then). I ran outside, but the lady was gone.

After I told this group of 40 people the story, I took out a two dollar bill and gave it to the coordinator and said, "This has bugged me for years. Here's your money." Everyone laughed. They loved the story, but the additional plus to it was that all morning when someone faced a difficulty in standing to tell a story, or give an introduction, the two bucks got waved around as incentive. We almost got someone to dance on the table for it. A stressful situation was relieved by that two dollar bill and the humour it generated.

Two of my colleagues also deliver speeches on humour. In one sense we're competitors, in another we're not, because we're strong individuals with our own material and delivery. I'm not comparing any of us to comedians or humourous entertainers, such as Dave Broadfoot, Don Heron, Luba Goy, Sandra Shamus, Bob Hope or Jerry Seinfeld. That's a different genre. We deliver information about humour, usually to corporations or organizations, and we're funny (on a good day. We're hysterically funny on a great day.)

Neil Muscott was one of the first Canadian presenters on the topic of humour. He's a story-teller and professional speaker; his words about humour follow:

> Laughter is an innate, universal, physiological mechanism that helps us fight stress. A good sense of humour can be cultivated, it's a learned behaviour and combination of attitude and skill. It's dependent on our environment and how we grew up. A sense of humour does not equal being happy. You don't have to walk around with a big smile all the time. It's very subjective—if he laughs at my jokes he's got a good

sense of humour. I think it's important to find humour in all situations, and give the self permission to have fun. There are often serious issues, for example, in a hospital setting, but people can still laugh. Humour could be verbal, although not necessarily loud, or visual, ie: something we see "strikes" us as funny.

The humour of inclusion builds a common bond and helps break down barriers; the humour of exclusion, that is, drawing attention to one ethnic group in a negative way, builds barriers. Studies show that people will approach their bosses more readily if they think they have a good sense of humour. Robert Half of the International Executive Recruitment firm in the United States reported that 500 of the top corporations in the USA were more likely to hire a candidate with a good sense of humour, thinking they'd be more flexible, creative and adaptable.

Many hospitals in North America have humour rooms now, such as the Princess Margaret in Toronto, a cancer treatment centre, the Hospital for Sick Children and the Foothills Hospital in Calgary, Alberta.

Resilience means trying to maintain your sense of humour in difficult situations. Being thrown a difficult situation doesn't just happen in improv comedy, but in real life. At times it's very depressing. Laughter helps us cope.

Another presenter specializing in humor as a business tool is Steve Donahue. Donahue suggests that when you're going through a tough time, you need to try to remove yourself from the situation for a moment and say, "Some day I'll be able to laugh at this." Now, if, as you're reading this, you are in the middle of a crisis, you may feel a violent surge at this suggestion, in the moment. However, if you reflect on what you do laugh about when you get together with old friends, isn't it often about some rough time? You know it's true, some things are funny now that caused you tremendous pain then. So respect the time factor, and periodically look backward in time.

Donahue suggests that in the middle of a bad day, you can write down your problem and mail it to yourself. The results are two-fold: one, it helps you let it out and, two, chances are when you get it back, you are feeling better. So knowing that time does truly help, helps you "get through it." Some other suggestions from Steve follow:

> You can build a sense of humour. Focus on it and try to do something once a day. Schedule fun—read a book, watch a video. Don't just stick a lampshade on your head if you're the quiet type, but allow the "child" within you to play. What did you do that was fun when you were a kid? For example, if you loved to ice-skate, but you haven't for years, schedule it in.

> Put a photo of yourself as a kid up on the fridge door. "Skip" to the office; break the mold in some way. In corporate tough times, it's important to celebrate small victories. Do anything at all—play music, slap high 5's, give out ribbons for making the deadline.

> When my son was born, he was so sick, he was close to death. My sister prayed for the baby, but she actually had the name wrong in her prayers, and I got very upset about this. My mom said, "Steve, I think God will know who we're talking about here." Fortunately, the baby lived, (and now knows his own name.)

I wonder about the expression, "I laughed until I cried."
Why is that? The connection between tragedy and
humour is very strong. In fact, the healing in crying
and laughing are both strong. Let the emotion out.
When I could allow myself to cry, I could laugh more.

Humour is a strong cathartic release. Get out of the house
and go amuse yourself; take yourself to a funny movie or a
comedy club. It will take you out of yourself for a while.
Try to get out of the obsessiveness of the trouble. It's sort
of like "whistling past the graveyard"—you're not at risk
and you can cope.

At the end of every skill section, I offer a brief summary of
the main points as "Skill Tips" that you can refer back to. I
also suggest a key affirmation that can be helpful for you
or a co-worker in shifting from a negative to a positive
frame of mind. Affirmations are one way for us to get
ourselves over the hump. They are positive statements of
self-talk for the soul. Repeating them can result in a more
positive attitude and improved outlook. When a person's
self-talk says, "I'm stupid," then he believes himself to be
stupid. The positive affirmation would be, "I'm smart
enough to learn new things," or "I'm capable of what I set
out to do."

Skill Tips

# Humour

1. Look on the funny side of events. Seek incongruities. Practise "getting funny."

2. Speak up. Share what strikes you as odd with others.

3. Read humour books. Watch comedians. Plaster cartoons all over the office. Send funny cards to your friends—and to yourself!

Affirmation

## I am able to laugh at myself and life's oddities.

> *"The trouble with being in the rat race is that even if you win, you're still a rat."*
>
> Lily Tomlin

## Skill 2

# How to handle the stress of change

Keeping a sense of humour and perspective is one way to handle stress, as we saw in section one. In this part, I'll explore stress in more detail.

There's no question that when crisis strikes, or even looms in the horizon, our stress level increases. We may handle one or two events, but what often happens is that crises come together, in threes or fours, and we become overwhelmed. So it's not just that there's a sick parent and a broken leg, but a close friend dies and our teenager gets in a car accident, all within two months of each other. Sometimes what puts us "over the edge" isn't the crisis itself, but "the last straw," one final item, perhaps even small in comparison, but that's the straw that breaks the camel's back. The neighbour running over the tulips in the mutual driveway can reduce us to tears or lead us to rage. It's too much. By itself it's very little, but on top of everything else, we lose the ability to handle it.

Many of us do have too much to handle most of the time. Certainly people dealing with a career, a marriage, kids, parents, house, pets, family, friends, that is LIFE ITSELF, have a lot on the go. We all tend to be in overload, in our fast-paced world. Add in an illness, taxes, commuting, dating someone new or no dates, a low-paying dead-end job, illness, change, lack of control, an unreasonable boss, reports, LIVING and we have a high stress level. When I have a lot of driving to do, especially on highway 401 around Toronto, I am definitely more stressed out. The back of my neck becomes one solid tense knot. I'm ready to scream at the other drivers, and sometimes I do. At age four my son asked if you're supposed to swear when you drive, but not at any other time. I had to laugh, and then watch my language. I'm glad I'm not commuting every day.

I especially sympathize with factory workers who are so locked into a specific role and schedule, with no ability to make a phone call or a dentist appointment except on a break. I once met a single mom who had to get up at 5:00 a.m., get the kids up by 5:30, make breakfast, take the bus at 6:30 to take one child to day care, a different bus to get the other to school, get to the factory, work a solid shift, race to the bus, go to the two places to get the kids, get home at 7:00 p.m. to start supper and get the kids to bed by 8:00 in a tiny one-bedroom apartment. No leeway, no help, no room for sore throats or complications, no control. That's a lot of stress.

Working for myself, I have often had money worries and no security, but at least I have some measure of control. Doctor's appointments, chicken pox (as long as it's not a seminar day, which it was once—thank heaven for a kindly neighbour), leaving early one day, are in my realm of control, or at least a modicum of control. A lot of stress can be lessened by more support for child care, elder care and leeway in the workplace. A healthy employee will always cost less and be more productive than a sick, worried one. Some companies realize this now and have support and flexibility built in.

When I was coping with single parenting a three-year-old, trying to get my business off the ground and the changes in my life, I was very stressed out. I had constant demands on my time, and no relief. My mother, sick with Parkinson's disease and in another city, was unable to help. Weekends were busier than weekdays, and I was not coping well. Add in depression, confusion and financial insecurity, and you get the picture.

While leading a Presentation Skills workshop for the government, I met Eli Bay, who was also one of the "stable of consultants" at that location. When he realized what I was dealing with, he suggested I come to his Relaxation Response centre to take a course on coping with stress. When I evaluated my stress level on the chart that indicates 200 is high, I was at 410 points. No wonder I was losing it. In fact, my usually healthy body was showing signs of stress. For the first time ever, I had developed cysts on my breasts and knees, and severe back pain. I wasn't sleeping well, and I had headaches and several bouts of the flu and colds.

During Eli's course, over the next six weeks, I learned techniques that I basically knew from taking yoga years earlier, but of course, had forgotten about and was not practising. Once a weeknight, for three hours, I received information and practised, with the group, slow breathing and stretching exercises. I regained a sense of control and calmness. I returned to a healthy state; all physical symptoms of my high stress level were eliminated. I was healthy, strong and smiling again.

Eli Bay, President of the Relaxation Response Ltd., Toronto, workshop leader on relaxation techniques states:

What we need to do is to get in touch with our recuperative powers, and coping skills. We have the ability to live in this world, in which stress is constant.

Some people are naturally resilient, but most find that the scale of change and events of our time give real challenges to our coping ability. The evidence is in headaches, sleeping problems, allergies, skin conditions, and asthma, which are all stress-related feedback to the body.

We've exceeded our ability to effectively flow with the current. We need to shut down the body's stress arousal state, rest, recuperate and repair. We can be like steam boilers, and if the pressure builds, without a safety valve, there's an explosion. The fight or flight adrenaline kicks in when it needs to, but if we have constant stress, then the low level anxiety is a chronic arousal state producing wear and tear on our bodies, minds and spirits. It's unrealistic to think you can escape from stress; it is part of the human condition. What you can do is choose to shut down, put in a safety valve, for a few minutes each day. Five minutes of deep relaxation is equal to four or five hours of sleep, as measured by the oxygen consumption and carbon dioxide elimination.

With practise, we can consciously put ourselves into states of rest, get out of our own way, to let the body's natural healing occur. We can withstand the pain and anger, become more adaptable, better in control of more situations and more optimistic, by learning to rest.

Ovid said, "He who cannot rest, cannot endure."

It's imperative we learn to shut down our bodies, minds and emotions for a few moments to recuperate.

## How do you handle your stress level now???

| | |
|---|---|
| Eat more food | Exercise reasonably |
| Smoke | Walk the dog (or yourself) |
| Go to parties | Listen to music |
| Sleep all weekend | Soak in a warm bath |
| Buy donuts | Get a good night's sleep |
| Gorge on chocolate | Visit a friend |
| Exercise excessively | Take some yoga classes |
| Keep frantically busy | Write the problems down |
| Shop 'til ya drop | Go to a movie |
| Get drunk | Take a holiday |
| Get sick | Breathe slowly and deeply |

Obviously the list on the right is better for you. Other ways to handle stress would be to join a self-help group. They exist for almost everything, from Alcoholics Anonymous to overeaters to shopaholics, for gambling, and so on. Call the local social services department for information in your area, or check the phone book. There is mounting evidence that self-help groups work well. People heal better if they have someone to talk with, whether it's a friend or a professional.

Some people think that if you go to a therapist it means you're crazy. The opposite is true; you're more likely to have good mental health by "checking in" once in a while. We take better care of our cars, sometimes of our bodies, than we do of our emotions or spirit. Just a few therapy sessions can be a big help. Sometimes we're stuck in a way of thinking or acting that is detrimental but we can't stop on our own. Choose a counsellor by personal referral if possible. It's the same as hairdressers—some are better than others, and some aren't very good at all. You don't want a bad haircut.

It's sounds so simple, yet we forget when we are stressed to breathe slowly and deeply. Just stretching exercises or, more specifically, learning yoga movements can slow down your breathing and heart rate to help you stretch and relax. Or, on your own, just get comfortable, either sitting cross-legged on the floor, or at the edge of a hard chair. Close your eyes and listen to your breath. Breathe in slowly for the count of six, hold for six, and exhale for six. Breathe from low down, the diaphragm, and not just the top of the chest. Then continue breathing slowly. Relax your shoulders. Bring them up to your ears then press them down as far as you can. Do slow shoulder circles forward for six, then back for six. Relax. Breathe. Slowly let your head drop to your chest, then pick it up again, and rotate your head to the right, then left. Repeat for six. Still sitting upright, relax your shoulders. Breathe slowly and deeply. You can do this whole series in five minutes. Open your eyes. Get up slowly. Stretch carefully. Yawn. Smile.

We also need to pay attention to what we eat. It can affect your stress levels. Charlene Day, author of *The Immune System Handbook* and registered nutritional consultant, states:

> When you are under a lot of stress, you should avoid cigarettes, coffee, black tea, alcohol, sugar, salt, choco-

late and MSG (monosodium glutamate, often in Chinese food). Try to find a substitute, or a program to "wean" yourself away from fatty foods. Another method is to have more of the "helper" foods, which are fruits and vegetables. Some people find pasta helps, especially if you're the "jumpy," high-striving, over-achiever type A. For type B's, the more relaxed type, pasta might make you too sleepy and you might choose to try more raw vegetables.

Don't drink cow's milk. The cow protein is too heavy for the human body. Goat's milk or soy milk is preferable. Leafy greens give you more digestible calcium and can relax you. Add a calcium magnesium supplement to your diet since calcium has a calming effect on the body. Try B vitamins, since there is not enough in our food.

We have a balance inside the body that artificial sugars throw right out. Sometimes if you crave something, it's because your body is out of balance. When we crave sugar, it may be due to a need for magnesium. Seek the advice of a nutritionist or a naturopath to find out what vitamins and minerals you are in need of. Exercise, talk to friends, laugh.

Resilient people are people who have an inner sense of never giving up. When the chips are down they'll find some strength from somewhere to continue on the road.

Anyone who asks for help should be commended. It's a difficult, but important, first step. You're not showing weakness when you ask for help, you're showing strength.

Some stress is necessary. If you have no stress, you're dead. Stress can be part of the spice of life. The right amount of stress (for example, a deadline to meet) can get energy flowing and stimulate us to greater heights. When the stress gets over your limit, practise these techniques. Get exercise, even if it's only a 20-minute walk. Talk to a friend. Put on a comedy tape. Read a novel. Soak in a tub. Have a good cry. Buy something new for yourself; even a new pair of socks can help.

Often medication can be decreased or eliminated by using relaxation techniques and a change in nutritional patterns. It's important however, to check with your doctor, who may be skeptical. You should never abruptly stop taking medication you're already on, but rather ease off, with a medical monitoring.

One time I was slated to give my speech on risk-taking to an international conference of pharmaceutical sales trainers. I was to motivate them to become willing to take the risks necessary to become more innovative. I had a pharmaceutical company as a client and had often wondered what would happen if people did learn to handle their stress better and thus need fewer heart and asthma drugs. During the break I spoke with two men, from different companies, about that aspect of the industry. "What would happen" I asked "if people really did begin to look after their health better, if they started to jog more, if they ate simply, if they felt so good they didn't need drugs?" Both men smiled. One replied, "It would be great for our company, because we make foot powders. Sales increase if people jog." The other man said, "It would be great for us too. We make birth control products. Active, healthy people have sex more often. Sales increase."

Unknown to me, I had picked the two pharmaceutical companies that would benefit most from people in good health.

Skill Tips

## Stress

1. Breathe long, slow, deep breaths for six inhalations, at least three times a day.

2. Go for walks often, take a yoga class, play a favourite CD at the office.

3. Take time for yourself, even if it's only ten minutes of peace and quiet.

Affirmation

# I am able to breathe in good feelings and exhale negative thoughts.

> *"I have a rendezvous with Death at some disputed barricade."*
>
> Alan Seeger

# Skill 3

## Allow yourself to "deaden" and return again

In her inspirational and moving book, *The Spirit of Survival*, Gail Sheehy talks about the daughter she adopted in 1982. Mohm was a Cambodian refugee Sheehy saw on a trip to a children's camp and was unable to get out of her thoughts. As a young girl under the power of the Khmer Rouge she had seen tremendous horror—the death of her family, people being tortured, raped and shot, starvation, children bribed into being traitors. Of course she "shut down" emotionally; how could anyone not withdraw from such scenes of brutality? Sheehy's book is, in part, about Mohm's slow recovery, from withdrawal to participation, from lack of emotion to feeling, from death to life. She speaks of "Deadening" as a skill for survival; so do many former prisoners of war and refugees.

I'm not comparing my life to the horrors of one who has gone through war encounters, but in suffering, there is no space for a comparison. If you feel pain, you feel pain. There is no scale in the need to pull back from emotion and life.

I've "gone dead" twice; in retrospect it was the perfect response. Once was when I was 18 and my father realized I'd been dating outside of our religion. Since he suffered as a child in Poland for no reason other than being Jewish, and since most of his family and small town were killed during Hitler's time, he had very strong, understandable reasons for his beliefs. I, however, was headstrong, smart, and in my first year of university; I wanted to date who I wanted to date, so I did. When he found out, he slapped me across the face, called me horrid names, and threatened to disown me. As a first generation child, this was extreme humiliation and excommunication. I didn't "go dead" then; it happened about six months later, after I had moved away from home to another city and felt isolated and alone in my basement apartment. I withdrew and felt suicidal for most of that year. I had trouble connecting with anyone. Fortunately, a friend literally dragged me by the hand to the campus therapist, and I got the help I needed.

The other time I "went dead" was when my marriage ended abruptly after 12 years. At first, I reacted strongly, by jumping into life more. I put off mourning or feeling much at all. I had a good time in order to numb the pain. Initially my ex-husband and I worked out a hybrid friendship. A year later, he turned against me dramatically, and all of it hit me hard. I spent the entire month of November and most of December crying in the living room. I'd take my son to daycare, come home intending to work, try to make business calls or write, and within the hour I'd be sitting on the living room couch, just staring at the walls. When I started to cry, I also started to heal.

Statistics show that women recover from divorce more quickly than men, with fewer health problems. I think it's because, in most situations, we have to get on with it, we have to look after the children. If the custodial parent is the father, then he is the one who has to cope and be there emotionally for the family. The parent simply has to get on top of things, function and get the dinner onto the table. It isn't easy.

I do remember the complete numbness. I felt cold, frozen in space, unable to move, unable to function. I couldn't look after the smallest thing. Everything was too much. But at 4:00 o'clock, somehow I snapped out of it, because I knew another life depended on mine. I would never, in any circumstance, want to repeat that numbness I felt. It was like being stranded in a dark, cold tunnel, where no light or time existed.

At first I couldn't cry, but each middle of the night I woke up feeling like a Mack truck was sitting right on my chest. I could barely move or breathe. Once, after such a night, I had to get up early and go to a conference to give a speech on positive thinking. Thank heaven for my previous acting experience, because I sure wasn't feeling the message that day!

A colleague of mine questioned my calling deadening a skill. Does one need to know how to go dead as a tool for resiliency? I replied yes, because if you've been there, you know how much it saved you. If you've had a real shock to your soul, such as a death in the family, or a business failure, going dead is a natural shut down by your senses. If you have sprained your ankle, you'd give it time to heal. You'd put your foot up and get some rest. Your emotions can be "sprained" as well, and need the time to rest.

Sometimes it helps to go dead on a much smaller scale, by retreating into a quiet state. You can decide not to answer the phone, make plans, or go out. You can give yourself a "mini-healing" by deciding to sit quietly. It's different than meditating or listening to music or reading a book. It can be helpful to really just sit still, draw your energies up into yourself, allow yourself to get time out from your feelings in order to be able to feel more fully, by choice.

There are different levels of deadening. You can pull back, pull in slightly, shut the systems down for a part of a day, or a week. If you've had a severe shock, you don't choose to go dead, it just happens. You might not even realize it, until you notice the difference when you are not feeling "dead." Often in a disaster, people are so shocked they deaden for awhile. You can see it on television after a flood, quake, bombing or fires. It takes some time for people to "come alive" again, especially when others didn't make it.

Les Beach is a psychologist and former college professor from Holland, Michigan. In his late sixties, he was able to volunteer for the Red Cross as a relief worker to the Flint River flood area of Georgia in July of 1994, after the devastating tropical storm Alberto. Les said,

> "The water had come in very fast. There was 23" of rain in 24 hours; people had to leave their homes immediately to get out. There were about 800 people squeezed into 8 shelters, thrown together onto mattresses on the floor, one next to the other, strangers in with children, the elderly, the sick, the disabled. Some were emotionally disturbed and on medication. Some spoke, some didn't. There was much stress and many tears, and then when we thought things were improving, there seemed to be a second wave of stress. One group seemed to "deaden" in the shelter;

they were in withdrawal and apathy, not doing anything, just wandering aimlessly. They resigned themselves to the mud and the mess, just waiting.

Others could see the damage and cope, and they began to leave the shelter for a few hours each day. They found things to do, from fixing houses to looking for temporary work. Some seemed to be in a "middle state." They didn't leave the shelter much, but they took pride in keeping their kids and their area clean.

The people who stood out for me were the ones who had a strong sense of community. They were articulate and seemed to know how to deal with people and talk with each other. Most people were just so grateful to have the Red Cross volunteers there.

As workers, we found that we had to "be there" for each other as well, since the work was so exhausting. Resilience, as I saw it in those weeks, is the capacity to recover from a severe blow or setback that bends you out of shape. One's past conditioning has so much to do with it. I'd seen resilience in action in my childhood. In my own situation, my dad committed suicide and left my mom with five kids, ages five to fourteen. She cleaned houses and did anything to survive, until she was able to go back to teaching.

She found strength in her religion and in us; we found it in each other and the community. We all had to pull together and work hard. Obviously I had some very positive modeling that gave me faith in the Universe or Higher power. I believe that we all must somehow look within ourselves for strength, dig deep and reach down for the answers inside.

It's always easier to "deaden" in the face of real pain or shock. That's what alcohol and drugs do for people—it's a way to deaden the pain and pretend it isn't there. Unfortunately, pain doesn't go away by being ignored. There's a lot of pain in large companies and abuse can be a problem at work too.

I often see a "corporate deadness" in large organizations. There is a lack of good emotional health, or even emotion, in the corporate world, because so much is based on appearance and staying in control. A few years ago I worked on Presentation Skills with a man who could not smile. It was tortuous trying to get some expression from his face. A former bank executive, he said he wasn't allowed to smile at work. He'd spent the last 20 years being expressionless and totally in control. It took tremendous effort on his part to allow his feelings to show, which, in turn, allowed him to make a more lively, interactive presentation, complete with facial expression.

Many employees are expected to be emotionally dead at work. Put in the motions with no emotion. Some companies don't allow their employees to personalize their workspaces at all. They are not allowed to put anything up on the walls, not even a "reminder to be positive" poster! How can any company expect its people to be resilient, take risks, become innovative or care about anything when the "people" part of the work equation is numbed? Often the most creative people are the first to leave, and organizations are left bare of the very people who have the capability to see things differently and experiment with new approaches to problems.

One person who eventually left banking to go into her own business is Franka Baptiste. When I met her I was struck by her regal beauty and composure. She spoke of her husband's sudden death, and I was curious to know how she got from despair to the calm strength she projected across the boardroom table.

Franka came to Canada from Trinidad at age 25, with her husband and two young children. During her 14 years in the banking industry, she moved up the ladder to the corporate lending section. At the same time, she also took interior design courses. By 1986 she opened an exclusive brass shop, quit her banking job and started to be successful. With five employees, her kids now grown, the future looked bright with retail and personal design work. That fall, on September 18th, their house was broken into and everything was taken. One day later, on the 19th, her mother died of cancer. Although Franka never smoked or took drugs, after five straight days of extremely severe headaches, she started to take Elevil, a tranquilizer for depression. She became addicted, and then had to go through the nauseating, sweating withdrawal symptoms to get off it again.

One year later, back on track, Franka's store continued to be successful. Her husband, Hollis, a metallurgist who moved into the construction business, was busy at work as well, restoring an 1897 schoolhouse and converting it into apartments. Their three children were thriving. Life looked good. On a Wednesday evening, Hollis went to see the project he was so excited about, staying until midnight. The next morning, after he left for work, Franka went back to bed, one of the few times she ever did so. A dark mood and eerieness came over her and she didn't want to leave the bed.

Knowing that she had to open the store at 9:30 for her

customers, she forced herself to get up. For the first time ever in 21 years of marriage, she did not make the bed. At 11:30 that morning, her husband uncharacteristically called the store to say, "I love you."

At 3:30 that December 15, 1988 afternoon, in the middle of the busy Christmas rush at the store, Franka called the construction site, just as one of the men was calling her. There had been a terrible accident; Hollis had fallen into a trench in such a way that he was instantly killed. Franka fell into an immediate "deadening" ditch of her own. She said that:

> When a spouse dies, especially so suddenly, there are so many issues at once, and you feel the impact financially, emotionally, socially. I felt guilty. Maybe I shouldn't have worked so hard. I sold the business in 1990 to take time to heal with my three kids. Eventually things fell into place. It's important to hang in there with the punches of life or someone or something else will knock you out. You have to stay there and take it. When I was seven, my father died suddenly. I knew about sudden deaths. You have to just face the reality, accept it. Where there is life, there must be death.

> After a sudden death, it's important not to do anything in a hurry. Don't change your life's course, it adds more stress. To be able to bounce back you have to stay focused on the life in front of you. No matter what happens, you still have a life. Get up every morning and have toast, if that's what you used to do. It might be all you can manage, but get up. Make the toast. Your mental state is not the same. Stick to the toast for now.

Eventually you will be ready to try something new.

The therapists I consulted with state that there is not really a fixed time frame for healing. It's natural to be numbed after the shock of a death. A person might respond by doing nothing or by sobbing. The survivor might "put off" mourning for a year or more. A friend of mine felt guilty for wanting to be sexually active so soon after her mother died, but it actually was due to a need to assert herself into life. Some children whose parent has suddenly either left them or died without warning might take years to allow themselves to feel, and move through, the pain, if ever. Usually a person takes one to five years to mourn, then begins to get on with it. We have to go through the stages of grief in order to be fully present in life, and ready to feel again.

Elisabeth Kübler-Ross is known for her book, *On Death and Dying*, and her counselling work with people facing death. She identified the five stages in coping with an impending death as:

Denial, Anger, Bargaining, Depression, Acceptance.

Steve Levine, a very funny comedian I heard at the Laugh Resort, a comedy club in Toronto, did a great send-up of those stages. He connected them to what happens when you lock your keys in the car (delivered with impeccable timing):

| | |
|---|---|
| Denial: | Oh no, I didn't. |
| Anger: | Oh hell. Oh hell! |
| Bargaining: | Please let the other side be open. |
| Depression: | Oh my God. |
| Acceptance: | Oh well, I'm an idiot. |

More proof for the fact that humour can help, no matter how bleak the situation.

It's important to deal with the emotion in the way you can at the time, but to get professional help if you are not getting on with your life within one to five years. Your mourning might include "deadening" for a while. Find one thing you can do as an anchor for yourself. Some days it might be all you can do to get out of bed and make the toast, but do it. Make the toast.

One of the tragedies that strikes me as the most difficult to recover from is the death of a child. It reverses what we assume is the order of things—parents die before the children do. Most people said they don't really ever recover from this kind of a loss; it's a matter of getting on with it.

As Caroline Middleton said, "No parents expect to bury their child." The Middletons got the phone call every parent dreads at 2:00 a.m. Her son, Aaron, just 21, died in a car accident. He was hit at 9:30 p.m. and died at 1:00 a.m. She is still bitter about not being contacted immediately and the lost chance to be there with him in his last few hours. At first she felt numb, but then got busy with the details for the funeral. With two other children, a daughter 18 and son 16, there was no possibility of sinking too deeply into grief or the others would feel the loss of their parent too. Her children needed her more than ever, and were always as important as the child that died; it was all that kept her going.

She kept feeling disbelief. Caroline said,

> My husband fell apart. I felt I had to keep control for everyone else's sake. You run on the fact you need to

be strong for others. I kept wondering why they call women the weaker sex?

My friends were very supportive. They allowed me to grieve and talk about Aaron. For some it felt too close to home. They couldn't talk to me, out of their fear that this could happen to them. The bottom line is I had to get through it. I did "go dead" for a long time. All of my emotions were turned to the off position, and I lost my sense of humour and wit. It took four years for some memories to come back, for me to remember Aaron's humour. I lost my excitement for things. Whereas I used to be so excited about taking trips, I became very blasé. It's been a long road back. In a way Aaron's death prepared me for anything else life could throw my way. I became more confident. I felt, 'Go ahead, take a shot. You can't do anything worse to me than what I've been through.' I knew I could handle anything.

My job was a safe haven, with friends who established a protective atmosphere around me, like a cocoon. They often physically stood close to me. Eventually I became more willing to try things I never thought I could do, because of this new inner strength.

My senior managers took the time to show me what I was capable of. Failure is not devastating or permanent; it holds no power over me. I did become more resilient, knowing I could always try something else. At that time I was the Project Supervisor for the Southern Ontario Library Service.

In terms of organizational resilience, I think we set a good example. With our budget cuts we were presented with the worst case scenario up front, so no one had to worry and speculate. Because we knew the truth, we had the tools to cope. People adjust and are more creative when they know what's in store for them.

We decided we'd all work four days a week so no one had to be laid off.

Little did I know that within a short time my arthritis would get so bad that I would have to cut back to part time and eventually leave. Even though I now have lupis and am in chronic pain, I still have my family, new involvement in the community and my sense of humour. I miss my work colleagues; they were always so supportive. I believe that resilience is the ability to cope with anything life throws at you without giving up. We are all so much stronger than we think.

Often music or art can be a way back from the deadened feeling, a way to connect again. David Sereda is an extremely talented Toronto singer and songwriter who emerged strengthened, eventually, after the death of his lover.

I find tremendous comfort in his song, written in the final moments of his friend's time on earth:

## Powerful Love

I won't be scared for long
not when I think about
this powerful love
that nothing can strike down
this powerful, powerful love.

I made some long distance calls
I've got friends
praying all over the place
but the crucial call is now
and I'm asking You
for a little more grace

and I won't be scared for long
not when I think about
this powerful love
that nothing can strike down
this powerful, powerful love

tonight may be the night
that death tries to steal
my heart from me
if he comes I'm gonna keep him at bay
with every atom of love
inside of me

and I won't be scared for long
not when I think about
this powerful love
that nothing can strike down
this powerful, powerful love

I make this long distance call
(long distance call)

out to the stars
into the core of me
into the hand of God we fall
Hands of Mercy
Hands of Peace

and I won't be scared for long
not when I think about
this powerful love
that nothing can strike down
this powerful, powerful love

Written by David Sereda, *the blue guide*, 1994,
Rocky Wednesday Records. Reprinted with permission.

## Skill Tips

# "Deadening" tips

1. Take time out. In an office, close the door and be absolutely still for five minutes. No door? Use the washroom as your quiet place, if need be.

2. Sit quietly, staring at a candle flame. As thoughts come and go, just allow them to drift by, without paying them attention.

3. Feel like taking a nap? Do it. Buy yourself a new plant. Listen to music.

### Affirmation

# I can be more "alive" if I allow myself time to be quiet and alone.

> *"Anger is a short madness."*
>
> Horace

# Skill 4
## Deal with anger

Anger is a difficult emotion for many of us to acknowledge and deal with. Often we fear it and its repercussions. As children, many of us were not allowed to express anger. Some of us saw too much of it, and want to avoid it. There are also some societal sex differences regarding anger. It's more acceptable, even expected, for a man to get angry and yell. A woman is supposed to bottle it up or shed tears quietly. He's in a rage; she's a bitch.

In some families, and cultures, anger is the norm. People yell and scream all the time. It's more acceptable, especially if there's love and then people kiss and make up. When it's out of hand, it's abuse, sometimes only verbal, but too often, physical as well. I cringe to think of the numbers of families that hit each other and their young. How many children quiver in their beds at night, hearing their parents screaming, or worse, hearing the beatings going on? This, of course, is not the healthy anger I am referring to; it's abuse. Abuse is out of control rage, and never, ever acceptable.

**49**

In this chapter, when I speak of anger, I mean the natural emotion to a specific situation, when the anger is justified. You have reason to be angry if someone borrows your car and bangs it up, keeps you waiting at a restaurant for two hours, consistently cancels plans at the last minute, ruins your new leather jacket, speaks to you with no respect, claims your ideas at a meeting are hers, or doesn't keep his end of the bargain—even more so if it's one person who did all of the above to you on the same day!

In some other families, anger is never expressed. Emotions are held in tight. You know someone's angry by the silence, not by the noise. In alcoholic families, the pretense of normality is common. No one's talking about the reality.

Often people tell me that they could never show anger. I understand totally. In my family, we might yell once in awhile, but basically anger was not allowed. My mother would sulk, or be quiet, or take herself to a movie, which would amuse my father. We certainly could never express displeasure at our parents. Once I yelled, "I hate you" to my mother; later that night I got the strap from my dad. My parents were European immigrants. We were to toe the line and show respect at all times, which meant no talking back, no swearing, no explosions of emotion. I was the model daughter until I was age 18; once in university, I began to see things very differently. I loved my dad dearly, and shared many of his characteristics: a love of nature and planting things, reading and learning, spicy foods and dill pickles. But we were both Taurus bulls with tempers that were slow to build but could blast once aroused. We went head to head many times that year, until I left home, in anger, not speaking, nothing resolved. Our anger and rage surprised us both, and it took a year to work back around to civility. Fortunately, before he died, we had a chance to share some quiet moments together, playing checkers as he was playing out the last days of his life, ravaged with cancer. He won the checker game, but died when I was 28.

Now I try to love my son as I wished I was loved. I try to nurture his self-esteem and encourage his emotions. Any emotion is allowed, but the expression of it has to be considered. For example, as a two-year-old, he could yell and be mad, but if he wanted to scream, he had to do it in another room, away from my ears. If he was angry, he was to hit the couch, not me, and certainly not someone else. Now, at age 13, he's learned a positive awareness of his feelings. I'm so grateful that I had years of teaching and being a camp counsellor so I have some vague notion of how to raise a child—and it seems to work. I still smile when I remember one perfect "camp counsellor" moment. The cabin of the 12-year-old girls was a mess. Yet again, the wet bathing suits were left on the floor, instead of hung up to dry. In my most strong 17-year-old newly authoritative voice I said, "You girls need to clean up. Enough is enough and I've had enough." A very profound philosophical statement if ever there was one. We all burst out laughing.

Anger is an energy that has to be allowed. Just as water that freezes in a pipe has the power to burst the pipe, anger frozen in us has the power to burst us. We have to get it out.

It's true there are certain situations when it's inappropriate to yell and "vent" but I question our assumptions about that. Sometimes the most growth and movement happen when we allow ourselves to show true emotion, even in business.

Anger once worked for me was when I was leading a seminar on risk-taking, change and innovation. One particu-
lar manager was making excuse after excuse after excuse.
No matter what suggestions and new insights participants
had, he would speak up and negate them all. Finally I
got angry and blurted out that if he really wanted to
change, he had to stop making excuses and start looking
at possibilities, and if he didn't come to the session to
do that, he could get out. I then called a break, during
which time a South American woman came up to me. I
was feeling that maybe I'd blown it by showing anger. She
said, "I am so glad to see some emotion. What is it with
you North Americans? I never see emotion." I thought I'd
damaged any hope of a positive outcome with this man. I
went to speak with him after the break. He said, "You just
did me the biggest favour. You're absolutely right. I've been
making excuses all my life. It's time I got on with it."

I don't recommend unprofessional explosions of anger.
However, I do know that sometimes that is precisely what
is needed to jolt someone else into changing. We can be
so professional, we forget how to be real. Most workplaces
have made it politically incorrect to show emotion at
all. Also people tend to take anger personally, when it
might really be anger with the project or the red tape and
stalling. If it happens that you feel angry, have some trust
in it, and let it be. As long as you clarify any misunder-
standings and stay around to help put the pieces together,
the real expression of anger can be the most honest
exchange to happen in a long, long time. At work it can
be helpful to say simply and clearly, "I am feeling very
angry about this right now. Give me some time to work it
through, and when I am clear on my reasons I'd like to
discuss it." If that feels too "emotional," try "I'm having a
strong negative reaction to this. How about I take some

breathing room and we meet later today?" Give yourself some time to feel what you are entitled to feel.

Of course, at no time is any physical violence tolerable. Nor is raging on and on, for no reason. If you are raging all the time, for very little provocation, you have a problem. But sometimes, a short outburst is necessary to clear the air. Angela Jackson, author of *Celebrating Anger* said it took her a long time to finally recognize, own and express her anger about the very tough beginnings of her life.

When she was six, Angela's father left her mother to take off with another woman. Angela's mother could play the piano and paint but she couldn't cope with her daughter and baby son on her own. She went from strong and feisty to relying on alcohol. She left the children, with no explanation or message, in separate foster homes. After six more homes, some time back with her father, and then with her mother (a serious alcoholic by then) Angela, at age 16, went to live with a girlfriend. She attended school and work sporadically, then got married at 20, but was a "lost soul" full of rage. In her words:

> I stayed alive on sheer nerve. I had all these feelings but I didn't know I was angry. I denied it. I kept everything down, all the pain and anger. I began drinking, because being numb was better than feeling the pain. Finally, after joining Alcoholics Anonymous, I stopped drinking. That's when I began to feel my pain. It was very difficult, but eventually it freed me. I knew I had no choice but to get out of the prison of anger.
>
> Anger can be a protective shield or a fuel that gives us energy and leads us to our creativity. I think resilience is being able to change, to go through a battle and

come out better. Some people don't make it. Neither
of my parents did. It would be nice if life was a fairy
tale. It's not. But if you feel the anger, then really feel it
and use it for energy; it could be the way through to
the other side.

Skill Tips
# Dealing with anger

1. Yell at a picture on the wall. Punch a pillow or the couch. Kick the bed.

2. Write a letter to the person about why you're so angry and cuss away. Pull out all the stops. Then decide whether to mail it or not.

3. If you are burying the anger with alcohol, drugs or sex, join a support group or see a therapist. Get help to deal with the pain. Do not inflict your anger on others in a hurtful way.

Affirmation

## I am entitled to my angry feelings.

> *"The ultimate lesson all of us have to learn is unconditional love, which includes not only others but ourselves as well."*
> Elisabeth Kübler-Ross

## Skill 5

# Maintain positive self-esteem

One of the changes in recent years that has affected not just income, but self-esteem as well, has been the complete turnaround of job security. Thousands of people are being laid off each day. From 1990 to 1992, 5,000 people in the mining industry alone lost their jobs, not including those in the related service industries. Many in Elliot Lake in Northern Ontario have regained self-esteem through re-education and volunteer work.

Several workers, such as miners, fishermen and women, secretaries, and factory workers, never had much security in the first place, but most of the professions did, and now that's gone. Three years ago, I went to Hamilton, Ontario, my former hometown, to speak about risk-taking and resilience to the out-of-work people who came to the government sponsored program. I expected to see the laid-off steelworkers, who were out in numbers. I was not expecting the large numbers of laid-off bank managers, nurses and other professionals. There is no longer job protection for managers, accountants, bankers, nurses, teachers, lawyers, and I expect that even doctors will feel the pinch as health costs are severely trimmed and more of the population choose holistic, preventive measures to ensure good health.

I interviewed one man caught in the restructuring crunch, John Woods, a certified management accountant. He began his work life at age 17, and worked steadily until he reached age 50. He did not take early retirement willingly, he lost his job. He was, like many men in his age bracket, with one firm, Simpsons, for 33 years. His company was part of his very being. Having been with one employer so long, with only eight years to go until retirement, his "game plan" was in place. Instead his company used him to restructure, then laid him off. John said he felt betrayed; his self-esteem and self-worth were affected totally. He got up at the same time each morning, put on a suit, and left home as usual, to go "to work" (really the "outplacement firm") so his neighbours wouldn't know he'd lost his job.

John says, in retrospect, now that he has work again, he was more fortunate than most because of the support of his family and colleagues. According to John,

> Keep networking; never let yourself sink into not making those phone calls. Don't get complacent no matter how rosy things are; keep in touch with people and the events in your profession or work area all along. When people lose their jobs their spirit is crushed. I was able to cope because of yoga, reading, walks and strenuous exercise. My wife and children were willing to cut back on our expenses and live modestly. One of the hardest decisions was when I turned down a job offer because I didn't want to take

less than I knew I was capable of. I believed in my skills and could be flexible, so I held out for a good position.

In my former job, I was under a lot of pressure and tension most of the time. Now I'm very happy and relaxed. I never expected it, but after working as a consultant for two companies, I'm now a financial planner and am really enjoying myself. Although I felt intimidated in my first new job until I learned the skills, I've continued to learn and the change has been refreshing. I certainly didn't feel it at the time, but really my former company did me a favour by ending my employment.

John's sense of self initially came from his accomplishments, skills and a steady job. Most of us have our self-esteem linked into the same arenas. One definition of self-esteem is:

"The ability to be good at something, to meet expectations and to complete tasks."

I prefer this definition of self-esteem by Gloria Steinem, in her book, *Rebellion from Within:*

"The conviction of being loved and lovable, valued and valuable, as we are, regardless of what we do."

She calls it core self-esteem. This is an important distinction, especially for people who do lose their job, or who are recently divorced or widowed and must redefine who they are in society. Many people who lose their partner feel they are "less than" others who have partners. One helpful phrase to say to yourself is, "I am loved and lovable, no matter what you think, say or do to me." It's difficult at a party when someone asks the usual question, "What do you do?" When you've just been "dehired," one way to answer is, "I'm between positions right now." A sensitive person will know how to respond. Or try, "I've been in sales, but I'm looking at a career change right now." The one piece of good news is that it's much more common nowadays for someone to have just been divorced or fired. You may find a more knowledgeable, empathetic ear, and even some good advice.

Catherine Mossop, a transition counsellor for 15 years and owner of Mossop Cornelissen & Associates in Toronto has an interesting point to make about self-esteem and people being fired. She says:

> A lot of damage happens to people's self-esteem before we ever see them. They are already hurting from their time within the company. It's relatively unlikely for someone with a positive self-esteem to lose it from being fired. They'll have a shock to recover from, but they'll recover fairly quickly. Even though it's now more common to be fired, the impact is still significant.

> In my observations, I see that men and women react differently to job loss. Most women seem to bounce back faster. More men have their identities closely tied up with their job title. They have a strong "provider" image to cope with. Men seem to blame others first, to go into denial, not admit they need counselling. They want to get out there, get another job and get going. Women tend to internalize their firing more. They're more likely to feel it was their fault, and they'll literally "clean house" first, fix a closet, fix themselves, do some soul-searching and then be ready to move on. If men

re-examine their part in their firing, it's usually after three months, and then it hits them really hard. Of course, that's not all men and all women, but I do see this difference.

Some people get caught in a victim mentality; they seem to enjoy it and get stuck there. Others are victims because they don't seem to know how to problem-solve, almost as if they were never taught it.

Both men and women need to learn to analyze the situation, put it into perspective, weigh the positives and negatives (without over-weighing the negatives), look forward more than backward, make decisions for the future, target, set goals and a pathway and make some choices. These are fundamental skills that so many people are lacking.

When companies are suffering and the morale is low, the employees begin to suffer from self-esteem damage perhaps two years or more before we see them. If the company is in trauma and the problems are not communicated well, or at all, it becomes a bad place to work. The boss undermines the worker, doesn't share information, shows a lack of respect—this is cruelty in the workplace. When a boss says "You made a really stupid mistake," he's saying, "You are stupid." Or his body language might say "You're not worth talking to."

The employee may not know what's going on, but he "intuits" it, and like the grains of sand in an hourglass, his self-esteem gets eroded away, bit by bit. This ignoring, negative body-language, lack of trust behaviour is harder to deal with than someone who is out-and-out racist or sexist at work. You can label that, and deal with it. The other behaviour is subtle, and very difficult to cope with. People with positive self-esteem would get out of that kind of a workplace, in a better economy. Now people have to work in places that can be very cruel, and damaging.

You might laugh at this, but my biggest piece of advice for anyone in a job loss is this: "Get a life!" It makes all the difference in the world. If you are so focused on your work, you're devastated when you lose your job. Volunteer, feel productive, get a life.

Our self-esteem is internal and must be carried around within us like a wrapped treasure. It can be attacked, and we may "get down," but the important thing is to "get back up again."

In my work, as a professional speaker, I have to put myself on the line over and over again, presenting to audiences of 20 to 1,000. I'm confident I'll do a good job, and don't expect to be less than an "A" rating ever, but want an "A++" each time. This, unfortunately, is impossible for a variety of reasons, from having the flu to meeting an audience that has just been told that moment by the company president that 30 per cent of them will lose their jobs within the month! I have to maintain my sense of worth, no matter what. I belong to the National Speakers' Association (NSA), and CAPS (the Canadian version) for support. Every speaker worth "their grain of salt" has had at least one "not quite there" presentation; we are used to giving each other support. Often the audience doesn't even know when we feel not quite connected, because of our professional ability to do a good job, no matter what. But *we* know, and we are able to discuss what went wrong and how to fix it with each other, so it doesn't happen again.

There are all kinds of scenarios my colleagues and I face:

Sometimes a speaker has tripped, stumbled or even fallen on the platform.

The audience was drunk.

The room was long and narrow and not everyone could see.

The introducer took half the time with his own "schtick."

The presenter beforehand went on and on and on and the meeting planner was too timid to get him off the platform.

Just as the speaker started the closing keynote of the conference (in a room with one wall of windows) a huge blizzard started (at 4:00 p.m. Friday, at a resort far from the city).

The dismal corporate financial statement hit the press that morning.

The college just lost a third of it's funding.

All the power went off or the fire alarm went on.

Twenty people stood up and left the session but no one told the speaker they had a flight to catch for a meeting in another city and had to leave that second.

The speaker beforehand talked about death and funerals (truth).

As they say in show biz, "The show must go on." We have to get up in front of the group and be "on," no matter what. So our self-esteem must be intact and that takes some doing. One way is with affirmations, self-talk, the pep talk from us to us. However, these affirmations can't just be slapped on top of some core negative beliefs that have persisted since childhood. It may take a few counselling sessions to work on some of the underlying negative thoughts. But for a quick boost or the beginnings of a desired behaviour change, affirmations are worth a try. They're sort of like chicken soup—try it, what can it hurt? Here are some sample affirmations:

1. I speak and act confidently in everything I do.

2. I am willing to be happy and successful.

3. I release anger from my life.

4. I forgive myself and others.

5. I am patient, kind and gentle with myself.

6. I accept myself, and others, without conditions.

7. I have meaning in my life and work.

8. I enjoy my healthy, fit and trim body (or accept my plump one!).

9. I am able to create new ideas easily.

10. I am willing to love myself and others unconditionally.


(My colleague Terry Paulson rephrases this one to read, "I confront and support myself as I would others," which I like a lot and is a great stepping stone to unconditional love—a very, very tough number to act on!)

To work with an affirmation, say it with your name, and speak in the present tense. For example, state, "I, (your own name), am able to enjoy my work fully."

A. Choose an affirmation to repeat to yourself, inserting your own name, three times now and three times just before retiring at night.

B. Make up your own affirmation that is particularly meaningful to you, to repeat now, at lunch, and in the evening, five times each.

We do have the capability to maintain a positive self-esteem, or to undo the harm done to us by others, and work at getting and keeping a positive self-esteem. It's vitally important, since it can affect every area of our lives, from how we speak to co-workers to how we relate to each other at home.

Nothing is more important than giving a child (or the child within us), love and a positive self-esteem. Author Dorothy Corkille Briggs says, "We are either in the construction business or the wrecking business." Who are you building up or tearing down today?

Jesus is quoted in the Gnostic Scriptures as saying:

If you bring forth what is within you,
What you bring forth will save you.
If you do not bring forth what is within you,
What you do not bring forth will destroy you.

Setting your own path, living your own dreams, loving yourself and others is essential.

## Skill Tips

# Maintain positive self-esteem

1. Learn a new skill, just for the enjoyment of it.

2. Learn how to use feedback and criticism to improve without tearing yourself apart.

3. Write out a list of all the things you enjoy doing. Keep it with you, refer to it often and make time for some of the things on the list. Maybe you can't get to travel around the world right now, but you could probably arrange to spend the day at the lake, riding your bike, going to a baseball game or drawing one picture.

Affirmation

# I am capable and lovable.

# Skill 6

# Visualize a better future

Some of you may have been to a "California-style" guru-led type of workshop where the main slogan of the day is "What you believe, you can achieve," or "If you can see it, you can make it happen." Or, on a tamer note, you may remember Kevin Costner in the movie, *Field of Dreams*, hearing voices, seeing old-time ball players, and holding the vision, "If you build it, they will come." He built the baseball field, and the old (and dead) players came and played ball. I have to admit, even as the inspirational speaker that I am, there's a part of me that says "Oh yea, right, give me a break."

Even with my extremely 'mild-by-most-standards skepticism,' I've seen visualization work often enough to believe in it. I have visualized parking spaces in big cities and found them, I visualized a house selling at the price I needed and buying another at the only price I could manage and it worked, against all odds. I visualized myself in the Air Canada promotion's winning seat and got it. Unfortunately, I didn't realize that not all the seats were to win free trips, so I didn't visualize the destination, and only got the $100. discount, but that was still worthwhile. I've visualized the success of workshops and books, and received it. (The technique hasn't worked too well for Saturday night dates, but that's Toronto and another story) Visualization works in many cases; sometimes it doesn't work at all, or not the way you might expect. I take my visualization with a grain of salt added, and I don't believe anything beats hard work and sweat to make an idea become reality.

To visualize is to see clearly, to have the picture of what you want firmly in your mind's eye. You can visualize beautiful open fields of green to relax by, or little space figures to eat the bad cancer cells. Visualization can relieve pain and aid healing, reinforce positive feelings or help bring about the change you desire in yourself or a situation. Visualizing unleashes the mind set that says "can't" to look for pathways to the destination, or at least to get us closer than we could ever have reached otherwise.

Often I work with teams to develop consensus around a group vision. We start with individual answers to the question, "What do I want?," believing it's possible to get it, and not censoring too soon. We then set goals that are specific, measurable and attainable, and set specific tasks to make the vision happen. It's an idealistic approach, but, with lots of discussion, creativity and problem-solving, the group is able to make the vision a reality. We already have more than enough experts to go in the other direction, the direction of giving up before we begin, of shortening the vision and giving up on dreams. Who hasn't heard "we don't have enough money, time or personnel"? In today's market, the excuses are often the truth, but who hasn't also seen things happen miraculously because someone was as tenacious as a terrier and would not give up? There's always a way to find resources; it's a matter of finding the way.

Kay Brett, a Toronto therapist, uses visualization extensively with her clients. According to Kay:

Studies show the effect of visualization on the body, of using images in our mind to create. For example, try closing your eyes right now and imagine a slice of orange. "See" it as you put it in your mouth, taste it. What happens is we begin to salivate, just from the image of the orange. To create a change, we can visualize it in some way, either through an image we "see," or through kinesthetics, or sensations in the body. If the image is just in the head, it remains a fantasy. We need the image to be in the body for a sense of action. If you imagine a new person coming into your life, a new relationship, but you're frightened of it because of a fear of the negativity, it will stay just a fantasy. The fear comes with visualization because the negative comes into play too.

Often as children we became frightened of a visualization, because we have such an unclear line between the imagination and reality. Children always feel they're responsible for what happens, so if they imagine someone they're angry with getting hurt, and he does get hurt, it scares them. We've become frightened of the power of the mind, so the anger and fear have to be cleared out first or we can't visualize fully.

I use visualization all the time. For example, one client was having difficulties at work with another person. I helped her first of all acknowledge the anger and deal with it, but then visualize herself having a different relationship to that person. She "saw" herself let go of the anger, reach out to the other person. It worked; there was a change of energy in the office that other people felt too. Once you feel it inside, it just happens, the relationship improves. There must be the conscious will to change.

Everyone in their heart wants to let go of anger and be in a positive place. It's so much easier if you can visualize the change first.

Excitement, enthusiasm, creativity and involvement can create miracles; negativity smashes them.

It seemed appropriate to me to include a vision company in this section about vision.

After ten years in sales and marketing with an eyeware products company, Dawn Laverdure felt as secure as anyone could feel in a fast-paced corporate environment. For Dawn, resilience means to see beyond, to have vision as opposed to reaction. Resilience is a business skill, a personal and business trait that improves direction and leadership. So, when Dawn Laverdure was given notice that she was pulled out of her section, into something nebulous called "New Products," she was concerned and shaken. She lost staff, and had no idea if she was being demoted or promoted. There was little direction and a lot of uncertainty. Dawn thought that she was really being put on the shelf next to the front door, and she'd be getting walking papers soon. For six months Dawn didn't know what her position of Director of Business Development meant—was she promoted or shelved? It took personal resilience for her to stay in the job without knowing what exactly the job was, but having to perform well from a very uncertain status. She said,

> For awhile I thought I was on my way out. Even though I was a Director, I felt like a total failure. My self-esteem was in question, but really it was my ego and pride. This was a slow death for me. Then I began to turn it around. What if this was really a great opportunity? What if my change was something good? People were watching me. I felt a fear of possible disgrace if I failed. I realized my actions would set their attitude toward me and affect my future. I had to act confident and see my own success first. It helped when I began to talk to my husband and to my boss about my fears.
>
> The turnaround started to happen. At one meeting, finally, my boss stated what a huge investment they were ready to make in New Business Development. I realized that their projection of anticipated sales, and anticipated performance from me, was very high. In fact, I had received a great new job. After his positioning of me and my department at that meeting, I began to get recognition from the rest of the company and New Business Development was given a high profile.
>
> But I won't forget how I felt for those five months in limbo. It took a lot to regain and keep my self-esteem positive in the face of "not knowing." When you're in a "vision" company, it's pretty darn important to keep your own head above water and stay focused on your own vision, and that of the company's, for the future.

There are two ways of looking at visualization (if you can stand the pun). One is visualization that you program yourself when you imagine your goal being reached. You "see" the outcome as your wish and desire, and you can set goals to achieve that vision. Athletes use it to visualize winning the game. Business owners use it to see the future of the company. Speakers use it to see the audience standing and clapping. Architects use it to see the project being awarded to them, and then completed. Most people who want to create a change use visualization to see the final result. "Keeping the vision alive" in the face of difficulty is what keeps most achievers going, whether it's climbing Mt. Everest, getting an on-site day-care established, affording a trip, buying that first car or developing penicillin. Jonas Salk, the inventor of the polio vaccine, imagined himself as a travelling germ as he tried to make his vision of a cure come true. You are in control of your vision. You might modify it or change it or mold it, but it's yours. You set it up and make it happen.

The other kind of visualization is receptive. In this case, it happens to you. It comes to you as a spark, a flash, a hunch, a dream, a knowing, or that little voice in your head. It's intuitive knowing: you know, but you don't know how you know. You get a signal from your unconscious, or your subconscious, just below the surface, that often jumps out when you least expect it. You can't program it; the intuitive flash occurs when it wants to. The key is to be receptive, and to begin to understand what it feels like when you get an intuitive spark. Some people get a tingly feeling, jumpy skin, a shiver on the back of the neck, an energy rush, a gut feel.

I'm using receptive visualization and intuition somewhat interchangeably.

The Oxford Dictionary defines visualization as:

something made visible to one's mind (not eye)

Intuition is defined as:
immediate insight by the mind without reasoning

I don't believe speed is the dividing line; receptive visualization and intuition are similar. Whether one gets the "flash" quickly or less quickly, or as a picture, dream, voice or idea is not important. The important aspect is receptivity and developing a sense of your own intuition, and when to follow it.

In terms of resilience, your intuition can tell you what to do next. Mine has told me when to move, what new topic to develop, who I could trust and when it was time to cut my losses.

Consultant (and my cousin) Martin Rutte and his wife, actress Maida Rogerson, are Canadians who moved to Los Angeles in 1989. After living through the Los Angeles riots and the fires, they were beginning to think about moving elsewhere. On December 15, 1994, as Martin was walking down the street in the middle of the afternoon, he heard a clear, intuitive voice say, "Leave L.A. by January 15." When he returned home to tell Maida, she said that she also "heard a voice" saying the same thing, "Get out by January 15." They are used to listening to their intuitive, inner sense of things. They moved to New Mexico on Thursday, January 14.

Three days later, one of the most devastating earthquakes in the city's history struck. Sherman Oaks was one of the hardest hit areas. Their house was in Sherman Oaks. They feel if they hadn't left, they might have been killed. As it turned out, Martin was back in L.A. on the 17th, for a client meeting, but he was in a hotel, 20 miles away, and safe. Nevertheless he said,

> I was sound asleep, then all of a sudden I was shaken awake, just as if someone had a hold of me physically, and was shaking me back and forth, only this was the whole building that was shaking me. I felt very scared. No one slept much. It was a shock to the whole system. Many people had no food, water or power. Some houses were standing, some just two blocks away were totally wrecked and condemned. A lot of businesses, such as restaurants and pharmacies, were ruined. Everyone was in shock. The good part is how everyone helped each other. I felt lucky to be alive and very glad we listened to our intuition.

The psychologists and psychiatrists who work with people after disasters say that often there is an immediate pulling together, but afterward anxiety and depression are common. Most people begin to get used to natural disasters. As one therapist stated, "We know we have to get used to it. We don't control nature at all." The earthquake warning is an example of predictive intuition.

Roy Rowan, author of *The Intuitive Manager*, makes a strong case for intuition as a necessary business skill. He says that,
" *...in all intuitive leaps it's not just the brilliance of the idea that's important but the heat of the enthusiasm that is generated...the biggest winners tomorrow will be those who can summon from somewhere deep inside themselves glimpses of the economic landscape ahead and intuitive flashes of the business opportunities that have yet to surface.*"

In Shakti Gawain's book, *Living in the Light,* she says this about intuition:

*"The true solution is to re-educate ourselves to listen to and trust the inner truths that come to us through our intuitive feelings. We must learn to act on them, even though it may feel risky and frightening at first...it is time to re-educate our intellect to recognize the intuition as a valid source of information and guidance."*

Skill Tips

# Visualization

1. Dare to dream. Ask yourself often, "What do I want?"

2. Be open to new connections and unexpected possibilities.

3. "See yourself" doing whatever it is you've envisioned, using all of your senses.

Affirmation

I am able to see a more hopeful future.

> *"...my business is to create."*
> William Blake

## Skill 7

# Be creative

There is a great need for organizations to be creative now, in order to respond to change, keep market share and develop new products. One of the most exciting on-going contracts I've had lately has been with CIBC, (the Canadian Imperial Bank of Commerce), facilitating a week-long program at their Leadership Centre in King City, north of Toronto. It involves the bank's corporate initiative on inverting the pyramid, values awareness, leadership and empowerment to promote its ability to provide the best customer service. Hubert St. Onge, former Vice-President of the Learning Organization and Leadership Development, who has since moved on to another corporation, in order to continue his work in Learning Organizations, was responsible for the Centre for its first three years of operation. He spoke with me about his views on resilience, creativity and the need to break patterns:

> To me there's a difference between personal resilience and corporate resilience. The first has to do with your own integrity. The second is about building a reservoir of trust. Both demand a strong focus, which I define

as vision plus the commitment and channeling of energy. I see personal resilience as the ability to work with a lot of demands. In a large organization there are many ups and downs, to's and fro's. Sometimes you or someone else gets hurt in the process of the work getting done, so we need to have the ability to regrow our strength.

My work requires me to be vulnerable, to have a personal energy with conviction. I need to work through people and sometimes that becomes controversial. It feels like two steps backwards at times. When I've had the odd disappointment, my first reaction is, "Why me? I'm just trying to do the right thing."

I think individuals mustn't become victimized by what's going on in the changes of business. Life is a matter of choices. We are all self-employed, nothing is permanent, so we must build our skills and know them well. We must look inside. Personally, I get up early to meditate, which I've done for the last 20 years. We recreate the reality with which we live; the internal creates the external.

People need a focus, values and ownership for themselves. We create our own destiny, so if someone is miserable they should go elsewhere, and that's fine, or they should work at looking at the pattern and breaking it. I feel people must generate choices and create their own destiny.

Resilience is about creating your own path and having personal and corporate values and integrity. By learning more we bring a greater capability, and by trusting more we build partnerships.

Creativity is the ability to see things in a new way. We are all creative, whether we're holding a paintbrush, writing a poem, finding new strategic alliances or trying to put a toddler to bed with no tears. It's the ability to match two formerly unrelated thoughts or ideas, to find new solutions that no one thought existed, to do things differently than before.

It's an innate quality, but it can be nurtured and expanded upon. Humour is one kind of creativity, and the surprise comes from the unexpected relationship. Sometimes creativity gets interwoven into our lives through tragedy. If children don't get what they need to survive, they can give up, they can make noise, they can steal, or they can ask for help and become creative to get what they need.

As one friend of mine said, after her most recent trial and tribulation, at some point you just have to say, "Screw this and get on with it." That's one definition of resilience! Some things just can't be changed, and it can be the ability to say the hell with it and get onto the next part of life that saves you. If anyone would know, Charlene would. Charlene Marshall is one of the most resilient, creative and life-affirming people I know. I have all the more respect for her because she started in the pits of life; it could hardly have been worse. Although Charlene's life sounds like a far-fetched soap opera, it is, unfortunately, the truth.

She was born to a mom and dad who got married at ages 15 and 16 respectively. Her mom dropped out of school in grade nine, was beaten continuously by her young husband who left them after one year. Her mom had three more kids, one who died, and a nervous breakdown. By grade three Charlene had been in several foster homes and relatives' houses, and six schools a year. She was left alone a lot since her mom worked nights, and was abused. Her brother and sister were taken into the care of the Children's Aid, but not her. She was resilient as a kid, able to transfer schools, make new friends and get good marks. She escaped into library books, but also into food and an eating disorder. Her imagination was beginning to thrive, and creativity was one source of strength that saved her. She used all her creative faculties, from a very early age, simply to learn how to figure out her life and survive. She literally created her life over again to have it become what she wanted it to be.

One Christmas, when I was 12, I took a cab to the Dominion store, bought a turkey, returned home, and fixed the dinner. My neighbourhood, Parkdale in Toronto, was filled with prostitutes, drug addicts and alcoholics; yet, some of these people helped me. One transexual, Susie/Johnny/Gary, regularly took me shopping for the clothes and shoes that I needed. I was exposed to drugs and parties. Often some guy would beat my mom up, I'd call the cops, then she'd drop the charges. I mothered my mom. I figured the more I did, the better she'd be. As a kid, I did the banking, shopping, changing the other kids' diapers, and the cooking. I didn't know how to do things; I had to be creative in order to figure things out just to live.

When I turned 17, I rebelled. I quit school, starting drinking and smoking, although I never got into drugs. I stayed with my friends' families, then I went "home" after a year, got my grade 12 and 13, and then worked three jobs in order to go to University. Once I got there, I had a real class conflict. I didn't belong. I had a double world. Other students were just getting into drinking and partying; I'd had more than enough of that. I finally left home and moved into residence with a friend, which "saved" me. Whenever I returned home, I was back into the thick of it, rescuing and getting no sleep. When this is your background, this is what's normal. It took me so long to see what was going on. My doctor, Marla Shapiro helped me see my family objectively, as dysfunctional and alcoholic. She became my role model, and I began the long road to recovery and self-respect.

I read everything I could about the adult children of alcoholics and abuse. Eventually I understood my background. I worked in Corrections, and then in Human Resources. I kept learning and discovering, reading everything and choosing my friends carefully. I began a more intensive health and spiritual program, to get over a bad marriage, a hurtful relationship, cancer and a job loss. (That's the short version; unfortunately, it's all true.) I am now happily married to a good man, I have a degree in social work, a full-time job and am expecting our first child. It's never been easy, but I have created a good life.

When I think of what saved me, it's that as a child I always had a healthy self image, in spite of very little love or nourishment. I had a grandmother who loved me and whom I loved. I have no guilt or shame about my past, even though I had to leave my family behind, for my own health. My friends are my family. I couldn't have made it without their help. Resilience is about getting back up again, not giving in. I have a "health wall" in our home, with pictures of my friends all over it. It helps me keep the human spirit going. I'm brutally honest with myself. Sometimes I want to withdraw; I wish I was less complex, more simple, but I realize I am unique. I have the courage to be creative. When the stakes get higher, my response gets better. There's a rhythm to life's problems. I come at things from so many angles, there's always a way to figure it out.

I'm a free spirit, moved by my spirit within. I'm more creative because I've felt the depths of pain. There's nothing I can't figure out. I felt that way as a child. My uniqueness, resourcefulness and creativity have seen me through. Now I work with women in prison as a social worker and am getting amazing results through trying innovative, creative ways to reach them. I will always have new things to try, new ways to create; nothing can stop me.

We don't need to come from horrific lives to be creative; I share Charlene's story as an example of extreme creativity, when being creative can mean your very survival. However, many of us are being stretched to the limit to find new, creative ways to market ourselves because of job loss, find new clients because of increased competition and redefine our lives without partners, or children or whatever we were hoping for. We can all become more creative by being open to new thoughts, new people and new experiences. We then must look for that unusual juxtaposition of ideas and trust ourselves to try something different. We must also be willing to make mistakes, take some risks, trust and become resourceful in order to support our blossoming creativity.

Skill Tips
# Creativity

1. Do something differently each day. Don't get stuck in either/or thinking, but try to see how to create inclusive possibilities.

2. Try a class in *anything*. It will increase your lateral thinking. Break out the crayons and draw a picture just for fun, without judging how it looks.

3. Create a strong, caring network of friends and colleagues to get the support you need to trust your creativity.

## Affirmation

# I have a natural creativity inside of me that wants to try new things.

# Skill 8

## Become a resourceful survivor

Being resourceful includes many different areas of concern, such as knowing where to look for help and who to call for information, and believing you can do something to change a given situation. It is also closely tied to creativity, intuition and risk-taking. However, I had never considered the ability to be resourceful as the ability to overcome other, stronger emotions to be resilient. It is for this reason that I decided to relate the following story here, because of the amazing capability of one man to put hatred aside in order to change from being a helpless victim to a resourceful survivor.

A few years ago I saw a one-woman show called "Punch Me in the Stomach." It's co-written by Alison Summers and Deb Filler, the latter of whom is the daughter of a Holocaust survivor. The play is about Deb's experiences as the child of a survivor, and about a trip she took to Auschwitz with her father. Unbelievably, it's actually a comedy. Deb is a talented, extremely funny, gifted actress who portrays all of her relatives, male and female, and their interactions at her father's birthday party. She grew up in

New Zealand, and is as at home with chicken soup and German tortes as she is with tea and crumpets. The play's title refers to an uncle who boasts of his firm stomach muscles (Go on Deb, hit me right here) and also to her own father's skills of resilience. Two lines in the play affected me deeply. One was, "I was a survivor's baby; I had to be strong and happy." The other was her father's, through her, "Make them laugh, Deb. You've got to get on with your life. It's all you can do."

I met Deb for lunch the next week to ask her about their experiences in more detail. She said:

> My father's a survivor. I have what is referred to in New Zealand Maori culture as the "fire in the spine." I'm a seeker, always on a quest, looking to try something new. In my youth I always had positive reinforcement of my talent, so I'm used to being on stage. It's where I can break through to the truth, connect with people, communicate with them and feel equal. I want to touch people, reach them. In telling my story I've healed my relationship with my dad. I'm very aware of being Jewish and what it means. No matter how many times you 'punch us in the stomach' we'll get up. It doesn't matter—Babylon, Massada, the Roman invasion, the Spanish Inquisition, the ghetto, the Nazis, the Jews will get up again. My being Jewish is an integral part of me, and the stories need to be passed on. The jokes are a form of resilience and culture, a way to keep us alive. I can't do just a funny show; I need to tell my father's story.

> My father was in forced hard labour camps from 1939, and then in the Krakow ghetto, and Auschwitz and finally Terezin until being liberated by the Russian

army in 1945. He was only in his 20s, but he survived. No matter what the obstacles were, he overcame them. My earliest memories of my father were in New Zealand, him shovelling bread into the oven, one after another after another. Once I saw him walk into a swarm of bees that everyone else was fleeing from. He didn't fear any obstacles; he'd overcome them and be filled with the wonder of how life can be.

So in a sense he was physically and emotionally equipped to be a survivor. You would think that when he was liberated in 1945, he'd want revenge or retribution, that he'd be overcome with hatred. The reality was, he had no time. No one had food. The Russian army came, the prisoners were free, but everyone was starving. This was only the first day after liberation. There was no food, but there was flour. My father told the Russians, "I am a baker. Give me the flour and some soldiers. I'll bake bread." The Russians couldn't spare the soldiers. So my father said, "Give me the German P.O.W.'s then." These were his captors, but the very next day, he was standing next to them, arm to arm, baking loaves of bread. He didn't spit in their eye. All he knew was they all had to eat, and he could bake. He had to be resourceful. He forgave them and got on with life.

I find this was an amazing lesson for me. I've come to believe that if you don't forgive, you'll have a hard heart, and you'll die with a hard heart.

There are many children of Holocaust survivors who can't talk about their parent's pain and how it affected them. There is a black box of fear inside that is opened for some, and left locked for others.

There's always a choice. As an artist, I'm more resilient because I'm able to be vulnerable. I do have something distinct to offer, and an ego and confidence that allows me to perform. There are huge swings. The part of me that's always challenging myself feels like an outboard motor. Sometimes it's unbearably heavy, it drags me down when I'm trying to swim. Other times, though, it propels me through the waves, I just go full throttle ahead. You have to give yourself the choice. We must be resilient, take risks and be resourceful. That's the exciting part of life.

I was shaken by Deb Filler's show—shaken by laughter, because it is very funny, but shaken emotionally too. Little did I realize that the man I saw the play with was also the child of Holocaust survivors. He'd never spoken of it, and didn't seem to want to much afterward either. I see the black box of fear in him, in the way he's held in emotionally, never fully 'out there' in his feelings. He never laughs too loud, joins in too much, feels too deeply, enjoys thoroughly. I recognize my own fear and story. It's ironic to me that even though being Jewish was so important to my father, he changed the original family name of Natel, to Nelson. He "hid" behind the Anglicized version, so I grew up with many of my friends never knowing my true origin. I also grew up feeling paranoid. Even though my parents emigrated from Europe before the Second World War, most of my father's family, and most the people of his small Polish town were captured and killed. I have a most vivid memory of a book arriving at our house. It was a history, in Yiddish, of the people of his small town. Night after night, my father read how his old neighbours and friends were taken away, and killed. He sat in the living room, crying through the evenings. I'd never seen him cry before. He told me never to believe it couldn't happen again. He cried because his friends and cousins and family had been gassed to death in the camps, their skin turned into lampshades and their bodies into soap.

I was about ten at the time. Is it any wonder that my reaction was to get as far away from Judaism as I could, that I married someone not Jewish and loved celebrating Christmas? I wasn't going to be different. I didn't want to worry about soldiers coming in the night. It's taken me 30 years to go full circle and understand the depth and beauty of the religion I was raised in, and therefore to accept myself. Working through the fear of identity allows me to be stronger about who I am.

Another memory comes to mind. It's ironic. A friend of mine married a German. When I went travelling for a year, in 1969, I went to visit them in Munich. I'd always liked Ann and Mike; we had many good moments and conversations. Then one night Mike asked if I wanted to go to see the concentration camp, Dachau. As a German, he had his own feelings of inheriting a culture that was able to systematically kill and run the death camps. The next day, he drove me to Dachau, and waited for me. I saw for myself the cramped wooden bunks, like slots for animals, a tray for a future slaughter. I saw the gas chambers and the high wire fences. I was extremely shaken.

I came away feeling overwhelmed that man could commit such an atrocity to man. I had a shame for all of humankind, that any one of us could kill anyone else, that only a few people spoke up and fought back for what was right. I feel the same way when I hear of a crowd watching silently as one person is beaten, raped or murdered. I like to believe that I would step out of a crowd to help a victim, but I don't know for sure. Do you?

Resourceful? It comes back full circle, to knowing yourself, what is acceptable and what is not. Who are you? What would you do to help someone else? What will you do to help yourself? Will you wallow forever, believing you don't deserve any better, or that you must relive your parents' nightmares? Will you be an addict if they were? Will you be a victim too or will you make a conscious decision to be a survivor? The first step out is always the most difficult one. To be resourceful is to be good at figuring out a way get to an end, a way to get out of a situation. If you are resilient, you are able to find help, from within yourself and with others. We all need to reach out and to be reached, to develop our communities and build relationships so we can be stronger together.

When I spoke at an Employee Assistance Program conference in Ottawa, Canada, there were over 500 people gathered to learn how to be an even better resource for their companies' employees in need of help. Some of the participants had a high school education, and became the resource for their company because Fred decided Joe should field the calls if anyone had a drinking problem. Instant "Resource Person." Others at the conference had their Doctorate degrees in a specific area, and were highly trained counsellors who met with employees to assist them in overcoming drug addiction, alcohol addiction, a difficulty in their family or personal lives, career advice and to maintain a referral network within the company. What impressed me the most was the obvious degree of caring and sharing of the conference attendees, and the amount of information available.

Forty years ago, there weren't many groups for people to go to for help. Most of the groups that exist today, exist because someone had that specific problem originally. An alcoholic starts Alcoholics Anonymous; a drug addict starts the Drug Addicts group; Candy Lightner, the mother of the child killed by a drunk driver starts MADD, Mothers Against Drunk Drivers, and so on. The person with the problem goes through it, and then decides to help others with the knowledge and information she's gained. The one in need of the resource becomes the resource. Being resourceful means looking inside, to find out what you need and then to allow yourself to be vulnerable, and ask for help.

Being resourceful means overcoming your own fears to take the risks necessary to get the help you need. Being resourceful means being creative, willing to try something new, allowing yourself to do something differently. Being resourceful means having enough self-esteem to believe you could be different, you don't need to repeat the mistakes of your past or your parents. Being resourceful means you stop being the victim and begin to be the survivor. If you have to take the kids to a shelter and be poor in order to start over, you'll do it. If you need more education, you'll get it. If you have to look for another job because your values are in conflict at work, you'll do it. Being resourceful means you give up hating and you forgive, so you don't die with a hard heart, or, even worse, you don't live with a hard heart.

What about companies, government, and associations? How can you be resourceful when everyone in the organization is suffering from cut-backs, wage freezes, overwork, and low morale?

One company that suffered publicly and had to change is IBM. For years this was THE company to work for, and THE computer system to buy. The "BIG BLUE" stood for consistent high quality. Unfortunately, it also often meant consistent high prices, and by the time it realized the consumers cared more for a lower price then they did for those three letters on their computer, it had lost a huge market share. Much has been written about the big blue machine, the huge ship too big to turn itself around in a narrow channel. The other boats were taking over the race. IBM realized it had to break up into smaller, more maneuverable units, and eventually started to do it. One of the people I interviewed was Don Myles, Vice-President and General Manager, Channel Management and Personal Systems at IBM Canada, one of the first streamlined units. In his opinion, he is more resilient than not, and credits his parents with giving him a lot of confidence and the encouragement to make his own mistakes. People who have a lower self-esteem and a lot of self-doubt find it more difficult to be resilient. He related what transpired at IBM in those initial years of major realizations, massive change and restructuring.

IBM was in its childhood, a 20-year money-making machine that grew like crazy. As one humongous company, it was basically at the whim of the person in charge. It became a victim of its own success, from 1964 to 1984. Then in the mid-eighties, when we thought we were adults, every premise got turned on its ear. Our problems, much like Donald Trump's, were needing to learn how to control the riches. When you are at the peak of your success you are the most vulnerable to the next trend. The impact of change was like the Berlin Wall coming down; nothing will be the same. Therefore the 20 year structure with central control that we thought could do no wrong, *was* wrong. It all came apart.

Unfortunately, it took us 19 years to wake up and see the changes that were needed. In December, 1991, John Acres, the former CEO disaggregated the company into autonomous businesses with more than one person in charge of it all. This gave us a better chance for the right answers from at least one aggregate company. By now the stakeholders' patience had worn thin.

I got one piece of the company to run with. I'm basically an optimist. You need to have high self-esteem, tenacity and resilience to remain optimistic. I knew that IBM would come out healthy. Optimism feeds on the self. If you feel good, the team does well, people feel good and then the company does well. I create opportunities for myself. I do what I want to do that's fun and stimulating, in order to revitalize myself. It's essential to find the ingredients to motivate yourself and others. In the 35 years I've been with IBM, I've basically only been "mismatched" four times. I would always seek a move to another environment, in order to remain optimistic and creative. I'm not the guy to make sure some procedures are followed correctly. I'm not an administrator. I'm a problem-solver. I like to be involved in the output, to take the best from research plus development plus people's minds and put it into something practical. I like to handle that transition.

There are predictable factors in change, not good or bad, just predictable. Anger and denial lead to acceptance and then positive action. Understanding the change curve is a technique for getting through it and getting support. As we got leaner and meaner, we had the support from our people, logistics and systems. That was a real shift and a test of resiliency.

Where there might have been three secretaries, there was now only one to do the work for several executives. That left a lot of support staff who were forced into change. There was the usual anger and denial. I think two things helped a great deal.

What I found worked was to show people other *possibilities*. Once people saw possibility and hope, they could be more resilient. Some women became role models for others. For example, one woman went from being a secretary to handling customer complaints. She did extremely well. Many of those people are now a treasured group in customer relations, handling in-house calls on the 800 numbers. They leveraged their interpersonal skills to move into outbound telemarketing and sales and helped our results.

I also became a *catalytic enabler* to get others through the trauma. I told people I would help them get through the changes as quickly as possible. They became prepared mentally to switch to a new format. Many of the ex-secretaries began to ooze confidence, and went on to make more money than before. I think it's important to let your people get angry, but help them through it. Give them new hope and possibilities.

IBM went through the "Valley of Death." Our problems couldn't get fixed over the weekend. We were resourceful; I knew we could recover and succeed. We broke the code of what we were doing wrong and it worked;

our market share is up, our new products are doing
well and this is an exciting place to be once again.

During the resilience seminars I conduct, participants
share their ideas for becoming more resourceful in their
organizations:

- Deal with rumours as soon as you hear them.

- Communicate, communicate, communicate!

- Get to the source of the problems.

- Encourage your employees; build their confidence
  daily.

- Be proactive.

- Find meaning for yourself.

- Encourage volunteer work and set the example by
  doing it yourself.

- Establish flexible work times.

- Create incentives.

- Seek out partnerships with other companies.

- Explore and restate values.

- Make sure everyone takes advantage of career planning
  opportunities.

- Look for, and celebrate, the little victories.

Any disaster brings out the need for the skills of resilience.
Some see the skills of "deadening," or creativity as the
predominant skill necessary. Others see a different skill is
needed, depending on their personal experience and what
worked for them.

One survivor of Hurricane Andrew saw the need for resourcefulness. Beverly Zucker, a teacher in the Kendall/
Miami area started to feel the effects of Hurricane Andrew,
which hit on August 24, 1992, around 3:30 a.m. The houses
shook violently for the next three hours from the force of
the winds. They were so strong they grabbed people right
off the street and tossed them about. As the winds raged,
trees were uprooted and debris flew all around. Beverly
stood in the bathtub with her daughter, her husband and
his 88 year-old step-mother whose attitude was, "So, I've
already been through so much. How bad can this be?" She
was amazingly peaceful and positive. Obviously some
resilience comes with age and experience! One ironic
aspect was that her husband Don, being very hearing
impaired, was less frightened because he couldn't hear the
howling storm. According to Beverly,

> You learn to do what you have to do to survive. We
> thought we would die for the whole three hours, and
> then it was over. We came outside to see houses
> completely demolished, trees torn right out. It crossed
> my mind that the trees couldn't fall twice. There was
> no electricity, phone lines, lights or police. Many of
> those in our area lost their homes and businesses just
> like that—all the family photos, clothes, everything
> just totally blown away. There was a lot of vandalism
> and looting. People stole whole new appliances out of
> the stores until signs went up saying "Looters will be
> shot." Some people were really traumatized, especially
> the children. There was a great deal of anger, increas-
> ing as the days wore into weeks.

> Initially people helped each other, sharing food, but
> then they seemed to get tired of it all and get aggres-
> sive. The anger had to be worked through. Eventually

people stopped being upset about being late for work and the attitude shifted to one of "I'll leave when I'm able to leave and I'll get there when I get there." So the acceptance finally set in. Then people began to feel that "As bad as it is, we can deal with this. We can not only survive and rebuild but we can make it better." There's something about having nothing, having survived, being dug out. You realize you're lucky to be alive. You have to rely on yourself and your inner resources. You can either call up on those resources or you can't.

Ironically, it was the survivors who were able to be resourceful in helping others who recovered the most quickly.

In 1993, Queen Elizabeth of England suffered through the fire at Windsor Castle, the marital separations of two sons and their wives and the demand by the public that she pay taxes. She was reported to have said, regarding her misfortunes that year, "No one of us is immune to suffering." Fortunately, she does have a plethora of resources.

Skill Tips

# Become a resourceful survivor

1. Ask lots of questions of everyone, use the library or the internet; get the information you need.

2. Think of six degrees of separation. Someone you know will know someone who can give you the answers, referrals and support you need.

3. Work at building relationships and community for yourself and in your workplace. If you are stuck in a victim mentality, begin to think of yourself as a survivor and build up your strengths, bit by bit. Ask for help. Forgive yourself and others.

Affirmation

## I am resourceful.
## Whatever I need is available to me.

# Skill 9

# Take some risks

When I interviewed real estate developer John Easton for *Risk It!*, his final quote was "Without change and challenge you might as well be dead."

After he saw the quote in print, he wanted to change it, thinking it was too strong. He did tell me those words and I convinced him not to change it. In the end, it's one of the quotes people have found most inspirational, even John, who said it in the first place. I interviewed 15 Canadian risk-takers, and I know I could have interviewed them again for this book too. All of them have also known adversity and overcome it. You have to when you're a risk-taker. However, I only chose John to interview again, because he had such a dramatic change in his circumstances.

He called me to say he was re-reading *Risk It!* and what he said in the book. Originally from England, John is a lover of sailing and Spain and the freedom to enjoy both. He had claimed that his possible loss of freedom was his big fear when he decided to start his own development company in Canada. However, he went on to become extremely successful. In the economic turn of the mid-90s, with the recession putting a lot of architects and designers out of business, he lost the very clientele he had designed one of his buildings for, and in turn, lost his building to the mortgage holders.

Being out of pocket by $5 million is not everyone's cup of tea. However, John's attitude was, "You win some, you lose some. I guess I'll have that freedom now."

Did he take his loss quite so calmly as it sounds? Amazingly, pretty much so, because John Easton has a strong, inner spiritual faith, good family support, and a full knowledge of what it means to be a risk-taker. Also, he has not defined himself by his money, so he has "a life" and the freedom to continue on with other developments and projects. In our most recent conversation, he had formed a new company to develop medical devices. He also has been assisting electronics and environmental companies onto the New York stock exchange. John's latest statement is, "It was all a blessing in disguise. I've had the freedom to do research. I'm working hard and loving it because I'm learning new things all the time. It's all part of living and risking."

Obviously, I don't propose that any of us set out to lose on the risks we take, no matter what the category or arena: physical, emotional, occupational, financial, intellectual or spiritual.

But all risk-takers know that nothing is guaranteed and a possible loss exists. All risk involves change. If you live in one apartment and move across the street to another, you still lose something. Maybe you gained an extra bedroom and a bigger bathroom. But you probably lost the morning sun and you preferred the layout of the other kitchen and you miss your neighbour. There's always a loss, even when there's a gain.

My definition of positive risk-taking is this: to take action for a vision when the outcome looks more positive than negative. Obviously, you want to risk when it looks like success is more likely than failure. Many risks look like potential failures to other people though, so one has to ignore, to a certain degree, all the soothsayers who say, "What are you, crazy?" or "No one else has gotten it to fly, Wilbur." In my workshops, I ask people to think of a risk they took that they're glad they took, and to then identify what enabled them to take the risk. For example, did you have so much money it didn't matter, or so little you had nothing to lose? Can your company afford to lose a million dollars taking a chance on the new product, if the potential payoff is ten times that? The idea is that once you get to know what helps you in your risk-taking, you can "call it in again" the next time you want to risk. Some common enablers are: confidence, support (personal or corporate), anger, curiosity, a powerful idea, an "I'll show you" attitude, and always, a strong vision or focus on what you want.

The "don't tell me I can't" thought occurred when I decided to self-publish the *Risk It!* book. Basically two different publishers were very interested, but in one case the marketing department didn't think they could sell a self-help guidebook on risk-taking (the book's in its second printing now), and in the other case it turned out the "yes-person" didn't really have the authority. So I felt frustrated, and that looking for a publisher was a waste of time, and that I could do it myself.

It turned out to be a fabulous money-making decision that also did wonders for my own sense of self. Also, if the person writing a book on risk-taking won't take the risk to self-publish, who will? What helps in risk-taking though, is a very clear sense of vision (I saw the need for the book and the cover in purple) and a very strong commitment to the idea (I knew people wanted *just* this kind of guide; they'd been asking me for it for years.). This is true whether the risk is personal, or corporate. The vision must be clear. Also, when you are strongly involved, you have more of a commitment to make it happen. I hired an out-of-work actor to market the book; he did a great job getting it into bookstores and eventually a large bookstore chain came on board.

Getting support is another key aspect to risk-taking. I belonged to a very terrific group of women in a "Wish-group," based on the work of Barbara Sher, author of *Wishcraft.* We each said our vision, brainstormed ideas and supported each other to turn the vision into reality. We were strong and gentle at the same time, working through the doubts and fears we all felt about our different risks. I'm not sure I could have proceeded without the support of them and some of my other friends who kept saying, "So, where's the book?"

In a corporation, it's critical to build the support efforts too. I have combined my thoughts with some from Peter Drucker and Rosabeth Moss-Kantor, to suggest that all innovation begins, like the music in an orchestra, with one flute player, the one solo risk-taker who has an idea and just begins. Then he joins up with another flute player, to begin a team. Next there is the combined wind section, making music together. The team learns to really listen to each other and blend talents to play together. Finally, there is the entire orchestra, making beautiful music together.

The risk is in the first stage, with one person who has the courage to come forward with the idea, the solo player. At different stages the light comes on, and energy is produced, which carries the entire sound forward.

There are many risk inhibitors, the factors that hold us back from even trying. These can be: lack of confidence, little money, not enough education, too much education (it's very hard for a doctor or lawyer to change careers) and a variety of fears, fear of failure, looking stupid, making mistakes. All of these can be turned around into positives, or minimized: "How much more stupid could I look?" or, "What's there to lose?" In a business, it's a little more difficult, (OK, it can be a lot more difficult!) but the principle is the same. The best companies understand that mistakes are necessary for any "out on the limb" try, but not trying new, risky, exciting ventures can be a risk in itself, by losing tremendous market share, or not having new product to sell.

No one group can afford to get smug; whoever thought that banks would be "selling" product, that lawyers would need to "market" themselves, that supermarkets would be selling specialty breads, or that car manufacturers would start to cater to women buyers?

The risks are there to take, and any mistakes need to be seen as "attempts and good tries" to go ahead and learn from. No one can move forward with vision if their eyes are focused on protecting their rear. The principles of positive risk-taking are the same whether it's personal, corporate or government initiatives we're looking at.

One area that's been so hard hit by the recession that it has been forced to promote risk-taking is the province of Saskatchewan. I spoke with Terry Crowe, who works in the field of Community Economic Development, and more specifically with Stuart Macdonald, a former Economic Development Officer in Saskatchewan and now Manager of Community Economic Development for Dauphin, Manitoba. They told me that since 1982 there was a period of very low grain prices and drought in the province. The price wars with Europe dealt a further devastating blow to the economy. Since the 1940s, there have been about 1,400 farms shut down annually. In their attempt to remain solvent, farmers spent very little money, unless it was for the farm. The move has been for the communities themselves to get involved with the economy, but without quite enough money, volunteers, support or expertise, it has been difficult to develop new businesses.

Therefore, one government program, the Rural Development Corporation, was formed to provide a five-year financial assistance and organizational support program and expertise to communities to help them develop their awareness, commitment and capabilities in economic development. The program would phase out after five years when the communities became substantially self-sustaining. Their motto is "Strong groups build strong communities." The plan was that over time rural development corporations could continue without government funding. Some of the new businesses which were identified by the RDC and initially seen as high risk and opportunity were waste handling, a machinery manufacturing company, food processing, herb farms, a hotel, a livestock show, breed testing, recycling, inland grain terminals and a cooking school. According to Stuart:

In Saskatchewan the people have been traditionally known as good farmers and good volunteers. These new businesses meant that Saskatchewan communities had to break out of the mold in deciding who and what they are. The people have not perceived themselves as risk-takers or very entrepreneurial in the past. Now there are a lot of contradictions. Some communities want to get out there and get going; others feel they need to get educated first, do the research and the planning. They need to find the balance.

I think risk-taking in terms of a community means that they "do the numbers" and don't quit readily. For example, they need to take risks to get the next meeting, do the presentation, make the call backs. They need to be able to look at failures as minor setbacks, not signs to quit. Look at options, plan, see the alternatives, stick with it. I believe communities here have to really think of being entrepreneurial as a matter of survival—where is the food in your mouth going to come from? We can't keep relying on someone else to do it for us, such as the government or the next door neighbour. I see that immigrants often are more willing to take risks because they know it's their survival at stake. They'll stick with it, work hard, and do what needs to be done. We must move out of complacency and believe in ourselves. Sometimes a lack of an education holds people back, but they are all capable if they'd just let go of some of the safety nets.

My message about risk-taking at the community level is that they must be willing to research, read, analyze and plan so it's not a waste of time. Keep trying and trying and trying. Value your neighbour; we are so interdependent. Then get out there and make it happen.

Terry Crowe would add that

really understanding community development is key to the success of the venture. Risk-taking doesn't mean throwing money at the project, but getting to the core of what's necessary, developing the project in stages and encouraging the development from the very depth of the grass roots.

All of which gets back to my key point of positive risk-taking: It begins with the individual who has the idea in the first place. The real support comes from believing in yourself first, and then being able to believe in, and be supportive of, others. Scratch any true risk-taker, and you will find someone who was told, "What are ya, nuts?" It's those ideas that fly. If it was so common, everyone else would have done it. However, believing in the idea and yourself does not eliminate the need for research and plain hard work. In the final moment, you have to trust your gut, be willing to make mistakes but then fix them. We are all insecure, floundering beings, pretending that we're not. So we may as well get excited about an idea, find the support we need and then take the chance. Life's too short to die saying, "If only…"

Skill Tips
# Risk-taking

1. Smile at strangers. Initiate conversations. Practise beginnings. Start suggesting your ideas at meetings and getting the support you need.

2. Sign up for something you've always wanted to try—guitar lessons, hang-gliding, t'ai chi classes at noon at the office. The newness will increase your ability to be open to new ideas.

3. Write out the "what ifs…?" What's the worst that could happen? What if it did? What could you do? Put fall-back plans into place, but don't get "paralysis by analysis"—act!

Affirmation

## I am able to go around my fear to take the risks necessary to achieve my vision.

> *"Life is mostly froth and bubble*
> *Two things stand like stone,*
> *Kindness in another's trouble*
> *Courage in your own."*
>
> Adam Lindsay Gordon

# Skill 10

# Keep faith

I've always been curious about premature infants and newborn babies. How does an infant struggle and make it when the doctors say there's almost no hope? Where does the resilience come from in that situation? I spoke with Dr. Jean Marmoreo, a family practitioner in Toronto for 22 years. "I am in awe of the strength of some babies." she said. She related the following story to me:

> This very healthy woman had a very uneventful pregnancy; everything was normal. At the time of delivery, a lot of bleeding began, which was not from the placenta or the mother, but the baby. Everyone was tense and anxious. When we lost the baby's heartbeat, we did an immediate Caesarian section. Eight people worked for 45 minutes to stabilize that baby.

> One and a half hours after birth we gave the baby a blood transfusion. It was in a coma for three days and it didn't urinate. The predictions at the time were that it was a severely damaged baby, unlikely to make it. Any baby in that condition—seizures, a coma, no

urination for three days—it's very unlikely to live.

The mother refused to see it. The grandmother begged us to let the baby die if it was severely damaged; she felt her daughter could not handle it. The father brought in his family, religious leaders, everyone, and they prayed and prayed. His faith never waivered. At the end of the three days the baby stabilized and recovered. It not only lived, it moved beyond healthy and normal. Ten years later, she is now a very bright, well-developed child.

We made a terrible prediction on that baby's fate, with all of our science and knowledge. There was absolutely no medical reason for her to live, let alone go on to thrive so beautifully. Somehow we did not allow for the infant's innate strength. I am in awe of that strength that was there at birth.

That baby reminded me that we must get out of the way of ourselves and others with all of our science, cynicism, biases, narrow thoughts, routines and rhythms. We do it to ourselves and to others with our science and knowledge.

I am in awe of the human capacity to emerge through pain to brilliant life.

No one would question that medical science has contributed to our health and well-being in so many ways. However, some of the old cultures of the world also offer innate wisdom that has been around for centuries and defies Western medicine. There are times when our interventions just don't work, there are times when it looks like all is lost, and the only thing left to try is prayer and faith.

Native culture includes the spiritual world in life and in healing. Healers work on the body, mind and spirit, recognizing that all three need to be in harmony within the self and nature to be whole. Edna Manitouwabi is a native woman and professor in Native Studies at Trent University in Peterborough, Ontario. Although others call her an elder, in humility she says she is still a learner herself, a fledgling who doesn't like labels. She told me:

> When you're in trouble, feeling hopeless and surrounded by darkness, you must try to keep moving and not get stuck or you'll sink into quicksand. Faith is a communication with a higher power, a way to an inner prayer, an inner cry. What helps is the tobacco plant, the sweat lodge, renewal through our children, dreams, all rituals.

> The tobacco plant in native culture is faith. It's sacred, something concrete to hang onto, something that will help you get out of the situation, help you see. In talking to the native plant I see everything that's alive. It is a time to sit down and share or lean against a tree. It's a way of writing a letter to the creator, your grandmother, your grandfather. All your emotions and feelings go into the plant which you can then throw into the fire or the water.

> Traditional rituals and customs also include the sweat lodge. On a spiritual and psychological level, it is like going back into the mother's womb for the mind and spirit, like being a newborn again. You can sweat all your baggage and burdens away, leave it, give it back to nature.

> The aboriginal people suffered many losses. Taking

our native children away and putting them in residential schools did a great destruction to our people. We were dehumanized, stripped of our customs, spirit and language. We used to have a respect for women who were honoured in their role of creators, so we had great respect for our Mother Earth and took care of her. There was a balance for men and women. One of our highest values is in our children and the family. We don't own our children but we do own the responsibility for them, to raise, guide, provide and direct them. We have to look at the pain of our history, to acknowledge the anger, hostility, self-pity but then give it up.

In native culture all creation is life; life has purpose, movement and is everlasting. The body returns to the earth mother, but the spirit continues. There are teachings along the way. The difficulties may give you pain, but the sorrow can strengthen you, give you courage. When you finish feeling the pain, you can say, "I won't be sad today. Today I will be kind to myself, because I am a worthwhile human being." This is our faith.

In one of my many former positions, before I finally began to work for myself, I coordinated conferences for Continuing Education at the University of Guelph in Ontario. One of the sessions that affected me deeply was on Youth Suicide. Suicide is the utmost loss of faith. There is no hope; the person feels only the darkness.

One person who has worked to set up a life line to counter the bleakness is Sheila Levy, a High School Guidance Counsellor, Trainer and Community Development Worker who lives in Iqaluit, Northwest Territories. She was instrumental in setting up the first Crisis Help Line in the North, a geographical area larger than most cities. Recently Sheila was the Chairperson for the Canadian Association of Suicide Prevention. She states:

> So many people see suicide as a viable option and the only way out of intense pain. Suicide is often the result of a lack of faith or hope. For people who feel they have no control in their life, this is one thing they can control; suicide is sometimes seen as a way to manipulate the situation. A suicide attempt becomes a role model to copy. It can start a cycle to get care but after a few attempts, friends get used to the cycle and things return to normal again. The suicide attempters then lose faith in the cycle to get help and then think, "well, I might as well just die."
>
> Often they want other people to change but they won't look honestly at changing themselves. The ones who recover and break the cycle get a renewed faith in themselves. They must develop the internal resources to become healthy. Many suicide attempters go from being high risk to no risk because they've learned they can rely on themselves and cope.
>
> Suicide in the North is a dreadful problem; it's a societal, social and personal problem. The need is in finding the solutions, seeing options and believing a change is possible. The way we learn to cope with our problems is the key to suicide prevention and healthy living.
>
> A suicidal person is feeling very angry and helpless. To help, you have to get the person to recognize and work on those feelings. You must let them talk about wanting to die before you can get to them to talk

about wanting to live. The person must have the permission to explore their potential death and to see there's going to be a hurtful impact on others. It's different for each person, but when I can see some ambivalence in the person, I can help him or her start to find reasons to live.

Faith is a power, a sense of feeling that a sort of harmony in our lives is possible. It can be a faith in the self or a higher power, whatever helps. Someone who is suicidal must find faith that things change. What looks permanent now won't be in five years; it won't have the same impact.

Recently I went up to Iqaluit to deliver two seminars for a Wellness Conference the city was putting on. It was an amazing experience; it is impossible to describe what the phrase, " above the tree-line" really means until you see it. It means NO TREES, nothing, nada, stark reality. I felt like I had landed on the moon. It was May, with a high of 0°C in the day time, about -20°C at night. The conference was for health workers, teachers, government people and townspeople; my words were simultaneously translated into Inuktitut for the large Inuit population. The first session was on Positive Risk-Taking; 30 participants were registered; more than 50 wandered in and stayed. We were to end at 5 p.m. At 4:00 there was an announcement for all of us to gather immediately in the auditorium.

Once we were there, we were told that a young girl, the daughter of one of the conference organizers, had hung herself and died. I was shocked. In a town of only 3,000 people, most everyone knows everyone. Sadness rippled through all of us and we prayed together. The next day the conference continued, beginning with a morning ceremony of lighting the seal oil lamp and prayer. The sense of unnecessary loss permeated throughout our souls.

Before I had left Toronto, I was already feeling tremendous humility about going to the North. What would I tell the Inuit, the people who survive the harshest climate, about resilience? Now I was truly humbled. I began with some observations, some information and then stopped. It was obvious more tears needed to be shed. We formed a healing circle, and heard from everyone who needed to cry and to speak. I was so moved. This was life at its harshest, its most cruel, yet the love in the room, the listening, the honesty, hearing their reality of lives lost on ice floes and in hunting accidents, suicide and plane crashes, alcoholism and poverty—it was all heard, held and honoured. We became very close in that room that day, young and old, Inuit and white, layperson and trained professional, female and male. Through listening, holding hands, honouring and love, we continued to shed tears and heal.

That evening I had a chance to go out on the ice of Frobisher Bay on a dog sled. We left at 8 p.m., saw the sun set at midnight and rise at 1:30 a.m., and returned at 3 a.m. I understood how going out on the land, sliding noiselessly across the frozen water, hearing only the breathing of the dogs, being away from everything, is so vital to the culture. All of the pain I absorbed from the day went onto the land. A big piece of my heart stayed with the people I met who are trying so hard to heal a culture bombarded by change; I will return there.

I felt a million miles and a lifetime away from Toronto and my usual corporate clients, but I thought that the need and value of people trusting, speaking the truth, and connecting is the same. I remembered one unique time at IBM when there were only four people with me in a workshop, instead of the usual 30. That was an amazing two days; we had the level of interaction I felt that day in the North. I'm not suggesting that workshops need to, or should, include tears and soul-baring to be effective, but there is a lot of room for improvement in the honesty of our interactions. The possibility for real connection is amazing.

I don't know how any of us can assume when we stand before the individuals of our organizations that these people don't have lives. How can we responsibly continue to ignore the humanity of our workforce? How can we pretend that the vice-president's father isn't dying, that the manager's baby isn't sick, that the supervisor's spouse just got laid off or the front-line worker is trying to hold his marriage together? We talk about work and lifestyle balance; we need to really listen to our employees, our co-workers and especially ourselves and try to find new ways to reshape our lives.

Of course profit is important—going out of business won't help anyone—but if we can increase our resilience, we can become more creative, resourceful and humane. We are not machines lacking emotion. If we can build responsive, innovative companies with people who feel valued, we can then take the responsibility and initiative to find new markets, products and opportunities. We need to build trust and have faith in ourselves and each other in order to connect in new partnerships for the future.

In the hippie days of the late '60s and early '70s, peace and love were the key words. The use of drugs did take the lives of some innocents and ruin the lives of others; it wasn't all a pretty flower power picture. However, the main principles of the time period reflected some basic truths and changed the fabric of our culture dramatically. We learned that we could come together in a non-violent protest, be listened to and promote change.

We learned how to be involved and question authority, how to speak up and have some input into how the world is run. There was less emphasis on material goods and more on loving one another. The spoken values of the '60s, before the distortion that followed, are very close to the core values of the Bible. The signal of a V-salute meant Peace, Love, Faith. Just words to some. A marketing ploy to others. But a real call to explore for many.

I would never have had the courage to travel on my own for a year if there wasn't a nomadic community of like-minded people to discover and travel with at that time. I typed papers in London, picked grapes in Bordeaux, worked on a kibbutz in Israel, and explored the market in Istanbul. I would never have had the courage to begin my own business without the confidence to trust my own instincts that my year of backpacking gave me. I would never have had the courage to do without money in the short run without that year of living with only the few clothes I carried in my backpack and making the choice between experiences or things. I would never have had the courage to continue with my natural, childlike idealism had I not seen it at work in the policy changes in government and education throughout those years. I would never had have had my faith in my creativity and intuition had I not needed it for my very survival on board a ship on the Mediterranean Sea and on the road in Italy.

Cynicism, criticism, sarcasm, judgment and suicide are easy. Maintaining faith, in a Higher Power, or in your own personal higher power, is difficult, but possible. To be resilient, it's necessary.

Skill Tips

# Keep faith

1. Wander into any church, temple, synagogue, mosque or spiritual clearing in the woods to sit quietly and ponder. Discover what helps you connect to your inner self.

2. Talk to other people who have been through some difficult times to find out how they got through it. There is so much we can learn from each other.

3. Volunteer. You will exercise your skills, learn new ones and feel renewed through helping others.

## Affirmation

The world has meaning for me.
I believe in my gifts and abilities
to better the world in some way.

# Conclusion

Love thy neighbour as thyself.

I always thought "Love thy neighbour" was the hard part. "As thyself" is much harder. When we can fully love, accept and forgive ourselves, we can fully love, accept and forgive others. Resilience is the ability to know there is more to life than that job, that new car, that spouse staying with you. Resilience is faith and the commitment to get out of the quicksand, to move with joy and passion, to love life no matter what it deals you, to find those to hold hands with on the journey, to love yourself and to honour that special, unique gift you bring to the world.

Resilience means you will get on with it. You may choose to sit in a plastic case, like silly putty, because you've learned to protect yourself a little. But you will also come out to play. You will take the first step, and live life as a dance, with passion and joy. You may stumble or even fall. But you will also get up and dance again. Twirl, gracefully or not. You will venture where you don't know that tune or those steps and be willing to help others in their ventures and trials. There may be pain. You can emerge strengthened. You are resilient. It's your possibility and right to choose to live, work, dance, love.

Life is a dance partner
Waiting for us to lead
With passion and joy.

# A further note on organizational resilience

According to Frederic Flach, M.D., Professor of Psychiatry at the New York Hospital—Cornell Medical Center and author of *Resilience*, organizations that are resilient have the following traits:*

Coherent but flexible structures

Networking possibilities

Respectfulness

Recognition

Assurance of privacy

Tolerance of change and risk-taking

Acceptance

Realistic behaviour expectations

Open communication

Responsiveness to new ideas

Tolerance of conflict

Optimism

Community

Empathy

Constructive human values

# How is your organization doing?

It is possible to take a resilience inventory and then work on the organization's response-ability. You can set up the structures to support change and increase the personal resiliency of your employees. As stated at the beginning of this book, strong, healthy organizations need strong, resilient people to forge ahead successfully through change.

> *"There is no grief which time does not lessen and soften."*
>
> Cicero

# Suggested books

Borysenko, Joan, *Minding the Body, Mending the Mind*, Addison Wesley, Reading, Mass., 1987

Bridges, William, *JobShift*, Addison-Wesley, Reading, Mass., 1994

Bridges, William, *Transitions*, Addison-Wesley, Reading, Mass., 1980

Conner, Daryl, *Managing at the Speed of Change*, Random House, N.Y., 1992

Flach, Frederic, *Resilience*, Ballantine, N.Y., 1988 (Hatherleigh Press, 1997)

Frankl, Victor, *Man's Search for Meaning*, Simon and Schuster, N.Y. (1939), 1963

Gawain, Shakti, *Creative Visualization*, Bantam Books, N.Y., 1982

Harpur, Tom, *The Uncommon Touch*, McClelland and Stewart Inc., Toronto, 1994

Hurst, David, *Crisis & Renewal*, Harvard Business School Press, Boston, 1995

Lauer, Jeanette and Robert, *Watersheds*, Ballantine, N.Y., 1988

Lightner, Candy and Hathaway, Nancy, *Giving Sorrow Words*, Warner, N.Y. 1990

May, Rollo, *Man's Search for Himself,* Norton, N.Y., 1953

McGartland, Grace, *Thunderbolt Thinking,* Bernard-Davis, Texas, 1994

Nelson, Reva, *Risk It!,* Words•Worth Professional Communications, Toronto, 1991

Rowan, Roy, *The Intuitive Manager,* Berkley, Boston, 1986

Segal, Dr. Julius, *Winning Life's Toughest Battles,* McGraw Hill, N.Y. 1986

Seligman, Martin, *Learned Optimism,* Simon & Schuster, N.Y., 1992

Sheehy, Gail, *The Spirit of Survival,* Bantam, N.Y., 1987

Siegel, B., M.D., *Peace, Love and Healing,* Harper & Rowe, N.Y., 1989

Sinetar, Marsha, *Living Happily Ever After,* Dell, N.Y., 1990

Stearns, Ann Kaiser, *Living Through Personal Crisis,* Thomas More Press, Chicago, 1984

Storr, Anthony, *Solitude, A Return to the Self,* Ballantine, N.Y., 1989

# Meeting planners

Reva Nelson facilitates workshops, delivers seminars and gives keynote speeches in-house for corporations, for associations, and at conferences.

She has been President of Words•Worth Professional Communications since 1982 and has mainly repeat and referral business. Clients include CIBC, IBM, The Society of Management Accountants of Ontario, and others in health, education, finance and international corporations. All of the programs have been researched, designed and lived by Reva and are uniquely presented by her for your group's information and inspiration.

For information or to book Reva Nelson,

call (416) 656-0994 or your favourite speakers' bureau. (Fax: (416) 652-8536/e-mail: revan@istar.ca )

## Seminar Topics©

Reva's focus, whether a conference session, half-day, 1–2 day or a week-long facilitation is on Communication, Attitude and Perspective. She connects with the individual within the corporation for greater meaning and positive results.

POSITIVE RISK-TAKING

RESILIENCE

HUMOUR AND PERSPECTIVE

MEETINGS FOR RESULTS

PANIC-FREE PRESENTATION SKILLS

LIVING LEADERSHIP AND EMPOWERMENT

MEN AND WOMEN IN PARTNERSHIP AT WORK (with Kalman Green)

## Keynote Speeches©

BOLD BRAVE CHICKENS (Positive Risk-taking)

I'M TALKIN', WHO'S LISTENIN'? (Intuition at Work)

BOUNCE BACK! (Creating Resilience)

WHEN LAUGH LINES MEET LIFE LINES

JANE AND TARZAN AT WORK

# Risk It!     *by Reva Nelson*

Couldn't someone you know benefit from reading *Risk It!*? It is the perfect gift for a colleague who's fearful of making a change, the executive wanting to inspire people to put forward fresh ideas or for a friend who's stuck in a rut.

Please send me_____copies of *Risk It!*
I have enclosed a cheque/money order payable to
**Words•Worth Professional Communications** for $16.95 + $3.05 (tax, shipping and handling) each in the amount of_____ x $20.00 = $_____.

Full Name: _____

Address: _____

City: _____

Province (State): _____

Postal (Zip) Code: _____

Telephone: (          ) _____

*Send orders to*
Words•Worth Professional Communications
58 Ellsworth Avenue
Toronto, Ontario, Canada
M6G 2K3
Phone:    (416) 656-0994
Fax:       (416) 652-8536
E-mail:   revan@istar.ca

☐    Please send autographed copies.

There is a discount for large orders:
25 copies or more—10%; 100 copies or more—20%; 500 copies or more—30%

Please allow two to three weeks for delivery. Thank you.